3⁰⁰

Aspects of

ENGLISH

HISTORY

CLAUD COCKBURN

Aspects of ENGLISH HISTORY

ILLUSTRATED BY

Michael ffolkes

LONDON

MACGIBBON & KEE

1957

PRINTED

IN GREAT BRITAIN

BY THE STELLAR PRESS

BARNET HERTS

CONTENTS

ACKNOWLEDGMENT

We wish to thank the proprietors of *Punch* for permission to reproduce those articles and illustrations which first appeared in their publication.

I

DELVE PATTERNS

What makes history tick so?

THE ASSERTION has been made, though without attracting any large measure of public interest, that the role of the historian in English history has been seriously under-rated, as compared with, for instance, those of inland waterways and women. It has been claimed that without historians there would be no history, in any acceptable sense, at all.

To examine this claim would not be beyond the scope of this study. It would, however, be valueless. The fact remains that, in the well known words of the philosopher Hobbes in another connexion, the existence of historians, as such, is in general 'solitary, poor, nasty, brutish and short'. One says 'as such' because it is true that, as mere living entities, they often continue to detect trends, conclude tentatively, lecture to students, and emphatically reject long after life has put, to employ a vivid phrase of the late President Woodrow Wilson, in conversation with the late M. Clemenceau, 'the skids under them'.

Not all, certainly, are to be classed with Diodorus Siculus, of whom it was alleged that towards the end he 'made himself ridiculous by deeming thimbles phallic symbols'. Diodorus was, it must be admitted, exceptionally unfortunate, even among historians. His literary style was poor and could not be used in school textbooks. Out of the forty volumes he laboriously composed, no less than twenty-five were lost without trace before many centuries were out. And, although he did not suspect it, later researchers were going to cover him with derision and contempt by proving that many of his stories about his personal travels and adventures were foolish and boastful figments, easily exposed by trained delvers.

Even so, and granting that Diodorus was, as the great Dr Jowett used to say, 'a more than usually false alarm', the casualty rate from theory-explosion, with consequent admiration-loss and neglect, has always been high among this section of the population, perhaps particularly so in England.

Many attempts have been made in recent years to analyse and explain the fear and dislike with which historians are so widely regarded even by those who confess themselves unable to account rationally for their repugnance. Among contributory factors one which was for many years probably *the main* cause of prevalent historian-fear, was the conviction that the secret purpose of history was to frighten people into doing what was distasteful to them, or else desisting from some attractive course of action. People who found themselves drawn to the way of life adopted by late and dissolute Roman Emperors were scared by news of collapse and Attila. Though our own Henry VIII evidently enjoyed much of his life, historians showed him as incurring more contumely than the average man cares to risk. The impression was created that hard work, discipline, and long sea voyages taken under conditions of the grossest discomfort were a recipe for success. The man who vaguely felt that he would rather live like the Prince Regent than Albert the Good found himself sharply rebuked by the historian.

In an attempt to overcome the prejudice thus created, many historians banded themselves together for a concerted move in the opposite direction. They put about reports that they were not trying to 'prove' anything at all. And they sought to make it an offence to pay any attention to anything bigger than a nugget of hard fact, promising, at the same time, a significant increase in the nugget-supply. This was to be achieved by employment of the 'deep delve' method instead of the old and – it was alleged – wasteful system of 'over-all range' or 'century grab'.

Users of the earlier technique thought nothing of starting out somewhere near the beginning of a country's history and simply trekking across it at a more or less even pace until they came up against the end of it. Others, using a modification of the same basic method, would mark off some century, *e.g.* the sixteenth, and soldier steadily on from '01 to '99, now doing some light delving, now surface-scratching, often making use of the 'comment' or 'appraisal' to lighten the work.

With the advent of deep-delving, this kind of movement became impossible – the sheer weight of the apparatus required kept the historian almost stationary. If he could cover 'Agricultural Wages in West Hertfordshire between June and September 1709' in a single volume he counted himself fortunate – and there is no doubt that nugget-production rose at a rate which previously would have appeared miraculous.

So far, however, as the long-term objective was concerned – the objective, that is, of overcoming historian-fear and the public shun-impulse – the results were disappointing. Asked (by the 1934 Committee of Enquiry) to what he attributed the continuation of his history-allergy, expressing itself in nervous spasms and scratching, a member of the public said 'all those mighty great piles of facts, and none of them really *meaning* one thing more than another, seem sort of eerie. Like if someone asks you how long is a piece of string,' he added with a nervous giggle.

Alarmed, and rendered, in many cases, almost frantic by the comparative failure of the deep-delve on which such high hopes had been pinned, some in their despair took up Universal Scoping and Broad Sweeping, using big, expensive Spenglers or Toynbees, according to preference, to cover the huge areas requiring surveying and assessment, for it was often necessary to move quickly from the Aztecs to Presbyterianism via Norman Sicily without re-fuelling. Others went fellow-travelling in what, as they too late discovered, were merely front-organizations for economists or crypto-psychoanalysts, and were soon either swallowed up completely by their supposed allies, or driven to quit history altogether in bitter disillusion.

It is small wonder that the public became increasingly depressed, moody, and frequently neurotic. The characteristic 'pop' of an exploding hypothesis, the high-pitched whine of a reappraisal coming low over the house, the crack of a definitive assessment, and the still more disconcerting ululation of an interim judgment being let off slowly close at hand, were enough to jangle the strongest nerves. And then the Dead Sea Scrolls imbroglio really, as one thoughtful Dean of Divinity put it, 'pulled the plug out and let public confidence down the drain'.

At the outset it had looked as though the historians, and their good friends the archaeologists, were, to employ a phrase, on to a good thing. They seemed to have a nice blend of nugget with broad significance such as any good doctor might have ordered.

Yet, within weeks of the discovery, the goodwill engendered, ('the feeling', as an observer observed, that this was 'more like history the way mother used to make it'), was dissipated by vulgar brawling among experts who seemed recklessly unaware of the overriding need to get together and agree on something to tell the public. People too far from the platform to hear precisely what was being said, reported afterwards that they had come away with the impression that the Scrolls might very likely have been written and 'planted' by an agent of Colonel Nasser, and that those of the experts who were not grossly and culpably ignorant were guilty of fraudulent conversion of meanings.

It was one of history's gravest hours. For, as the same observer whose observation has already been quoted, observed later – and by this time it was somewhat more of an animadversion than an observation – 'if they can foul up a thing like this, what price Magna Carta?' And his alarm was generally felt to be justified.

It was just the kind of thing to intensify in the public mind what is known to psychiatrists as the Anthony à Wood reaction, with reference to remarks made about antiquary and historian John Aubrey (1626-1697 probably, unless there is some error in the records) by his fellow-delver Anthony à Wood. Although in this case both men were in a sense historians, the situation was a typical historian-public relationship, with Wood in the position of the public. Aubrey was supposed to be feeding him a supply of useful historical facts upon which Wood hoped to rely in forming a considered view of whatever had been going on. Keen Aubrey (too keen, some wilier historians might estimate) took it as axiomatic that leading figures, statesmen, earls, bishops, scientists, and influential belles and beauties are apt to be tight-lipped of a morning, and do not really make with the disclosures and the indiscretions until at least partially drunk. He toured about from country house to country house, and night after night sat up with the informed insiders, drinking like a fish. Many times, the furniture – Jacobean at that – swung so that he hardly knew whether what they were fascinatingly reminiscing about was the world première of *Hamlet* or the battle of Nazeby.

Later, he had to get off the floor, snatch a few hours of troubled sleep, and start writing a yard or two of history for eager Wood. Naturally, like any other historian, he got a good many things – dates, names of treacherous intriguers, who seduced whom when – mixed up and wrong. Wood, taking it all as certified and attested history, spread abroad a bit of it, to the effect that if anyone supposed the Earl of Clarendon to have been, in his judicial capacity, as incorruptible as people would like judges to be, it might be worth while to take a look at this little deal and that little deal. They prosecuted Wood for defamation, and when Aubrey said 'Well, that's what I thought the man said happened, but of course I had no time to check the story, and in any case everyone was pretty high at the time, you know what things are', Wood, who was now in for a bad session with the authorities, jail looming, wrote a harsh word.

'He', wrote Wood, referring to Aubrey, 'was a shiftless person, roving and magotie-headed, and sometimes little better than crased. And, being exceedingly credulous, would stuff his many letters with follies and misinformations which sometimes would guide him' *i.e.* public Wood 'into the paths of errour.'

No one cares to be led into paths of error, let alone prosecuted, just merely on account of over-confidence in historians, especially as there is no way of telling which of them were drunk at the moment when they were purporting to take that long, fresh look at the economic policy of Henry III. That is why the Wood reaction is a vitally sensitive test. Does a given reader, in other words, trust his historian, or does he not? Without mutual confidence, not far can be got, even in the case of what is termed 'sub' or 'just-the-other-day' history where the historian starts by claiming that a funny thing happened to him on his way to the lecture hall – he found out the truth about Mussolini or Admiral Canaris or Stalin or someone.

The fact is that if an historian starts worrying too much about whether he is misleading the reader, giving the world, as the second Lord Salisbury used to say, 'a bum steer', he will probably never write another line, leaving the citizenry with a nasty void extending right up to yesterday evening's newspaper.

This is a mistake which this series of studies has sought to avoid. Where, for example, it seems desirable to assert that something happened because if it had happened that would be encouraging to some movement of our own day deemed desirable by the historian – as for instance, we could hardly have had the public schools had not somebody forged a picture of the Roman Republic and its virtues, so worthy of imitation – such assertions will be made without fear or favour.

When deep-delving is called for (and there is ground for the belief that there is still plenty of dirt where the rest came from), the reader may be assured that the best delvers have been chartered for the purpose. Nor will there be found here any inhibition against flights of fancy, judgments which might better have been left in abeyance, factual inaccuracies or bias.

For whatever, after all, may be said of the web of English history, cannot these be seen when we look back over the tradition-sodden years, as its woof?

II

THE EDGES

One view of mammoths

IT HAS BEEN WELL SAID by a little known leader of the Trades Union Congress that the 'history of England is, essentially, the history of the rural, urban and suburban districts of the area with, it is scarcely necessary to add, that of their inhabitants, existing under different conditions at different times'.

This is sound doctrine, and the historian can only regret that the speaker did not amplify his statement by pointing out that such a definition must include islands fairly close to the coast. It cannot be too strongly emphasized that any attempt to 'see' English history in the round, while neglecting the islands of Anglesey, Canvey, and Wight, is foredoomed to failure.

There were coloured cliffs at Alum Bay long before civilization, with its ideas, golf courses, hopes, fears and so on was thought of, and rightly so. Dinosaurs may well have been there too. Mammoths, in a state of almost complete preservation, some of them with grass still in their mouths, have not been unearthed in the region. And their absence has averted – in a manner which many have found characteristic of the English genius –

a good deal of strife, controversy and internecine row about how this thing happened to them.

Siberia was less fortunate.

The point, moot in any case, does little or nothing to answer the questions to which all history tends, or should tend, namely:

(*a*) How did we, non-mammoths, get where we are?

(*b*) Where do we suppose we are going?

The individual who is disposed to reply to question (*a*) that one may 'search' him, and to question (*b*) 'to hell in a handcart' is not viewing the situation in the light of the plenitude of modern knowledge – though, as any responsible historian must admit, the extent of knowledge is merely another way of expressing the extent of ignorance.

Those who, on the other hand, arbitrarily divide our history into the enclosure period, the disclosure period and the current foreclosure period, are underestimating the significance not only of the early Education Acts, the early Rent Restriction Acts, the early Defence of the Realm Acts and Toynbee's law, but also of the Taff Vale judgment, the Ebbw Vale judgment and – in the wider sense – Wales.

These were turning points. An historian may easily miss the significance of a couple of them – 'sort of thing', as Professor Schlau of Chicago was wont to put it, 'might happen to anyone' – but he who misses five in a row may well ask himself whether he might not be better occupied in some other form of gainful employment.

It is equally important for the student to realize that

whereas until fairly recently it was known that whatever was supposed to have happened had not happened – at least not in that form – it is now known that it did happen after all.

The Black Death, for example, was not – as so many brought up in the old-fashioned public schools were taught to believe – a mild form of influenza grossly exaggerated by excitable chroniclers. It was the Black Death. The same is true of Druids. They were there, with altars, as had been originally supposed. People who sought to ease them off the historical map with a suggestion that they had become confused with another cult altogether have been forced to withdraw unreservedly.

There are, of course, variations between their behaviour-patterns and our own. We do not, for example, cut the throats of maidens on rock-altars at sun-up on midsummer's day. They did. It is an essential difference in pattern. On the other hand though one may sympathize with those who argue that the Druid clergy 'got results', whereas pews are empty in many a modern church, this is not the whole story. Some historians hold that the Druids were – to use a neologism – 'feather-bedded' by the Celtic State to a degree which a curate of our day might envy.

The point which more nearly concerns us of mid-twentieth century England is that they were, as Shivac underlines in his 'Sea-surroundedness as a factor in folk-environmental development', already 'group-identified.' Their 'action-formulae' were well established, though in a mould different from those of – say – a Rotarian or Treasury official of the present day. History is, after all, not so much a thing as a process – a fact sufficiently indicated by such dynamic events as the rise of nationalism, the rise of capitalism, the rise of communism, the rise of the Labour Party and the rise – no less remarkable in its quiet way – in the cost of living.

'Things seem to be looking up all round', the late Lord Balfour is reported to have observed in his inimitable fashion when they brought him the news.

It will be necessary to consider in later chapters the fairly long period between the disestablishment of the Druids (many of whom were, in any case, Irish and had ceased to command popular confidence) and the year of the Great Exhibition in 1851. Nor did what may properly be called 'English history' stop there. On the contrary, its development can be traced in clear line through the Early Days of Motoring and the Early Closing Act, right up to Earl Attlee.

The position of the villeins, the incidence of quit-rents, fiefs, and the Elizabethan Age are all relevant to what came after. The period is a difficult one, partly because so many of its records are written in language almost unintelligible to the modern reader. Also wars, some of them even civil, often held up the ordinary development of social, and what later came to be termed 'economic' life. We must also, in fairness to the period, take into account the fact that almost everyone was either somewhat drunk most of the time or sickening for a bad case of typhus.

It was not until the *Encyclopaedia Britannica* drew attention to the composition of such liquors as mead, mulsum and metheglin (a cocktail made of fermented honey and wine, spiked with Welsh drugs, and strong enough to blow the top of the average villein's head off) that there began to be any true understanding of what they were all up against.

Fleibitz, of the University of Michigan in his 'Reconstruction of alcohol-intake patterns of the middle English', estimates that the liquor Queen Elizabeth took daily with her breakfast steak alone was the alcoholic equivalent of a half bottle of any good brand of whisky.

The alternative for one and all was to quaff badly infected water. And this was the case not only at breakfast, but at the mid-morning break, at lunch, at afternoon mead, and at dinner. Naturally most people preferred to be permanently pickled in wine, mead or other powerful liquors.

This explains much that at one time brought the period into disrepute. In the circumstances, no one could be seriously censured for being drunk in charge of a war horse, galleon, or the Privy Purse. And if Shakespeare (another case, incidentally, of someone who is now thought to have really happened instead of being an Italian monk in the service of the Earl of Leicester) often wrote a lot of high-faluting nonsense, this was due simply to something he drank.

The whole situation admirably illustrates a major difficulty of the historian which must always be that of maintaining an objective balance, trying not to imply – even in a footnote – that one thing is worse than another.

Professor Zenkoroff, of the University of Kansas, once confessed, in a personal letter to a friend, that he 'hated the guts of the thirteenth century'. He said he would 'get the goods on it if it's the last thing I do'. He added that were he not convinced that the facts were enough to damn the thing anyway, he would be tempted to 'slip a little something into the record'.

Even in a public lecture, when asked by a student a question about Simon de Montfort, he permitted himself to reply 'Listen, you want to know something about that so-and-so? All right, so I'll tell you, but it isn't going to be pretty'.

Such an attitude in a distinguished scholar must be deplored, the more so as it is not uncommon. The nineteenth century suffered from it for a good many years after it was over, and thus precluded from defending itself. The attacks, though for this reason in the worst possible taste, found a certain justification in the reckless over-production of Tennyson and unpleasant incidents towards the close, such as the Tranby Croft case.

Even the twentieth century has not always escaped the ill-natured jibes of men who may truly be said to be 'friends of every century but their own'.

III

A TREND

How money came about

ALL THAT ONE CAN SAY', says G. M. Trevelyan on page 96 of his *English Social History*, 'is that, in the thirteenth century, English thought and society were medieval, and in the nineteenth century they were not'.

Daring as the statement may appear, the writer was Master of Trinity College at the time, and his estimate, though pungently expressed, has the ring of truth. Indeed, one might take it a step further and assert that, with certain qualifications, English thought and society in the mid-twentieth century differed, in numerous aspects, from the thought and society of the Victorian period.

The inflation of the penumatic tyre, the deflation of the ego, and the inflation of inflation *per se*, had brought about a levelling 'up', accompanied by a levelling 'down', as a result of which it was possible to demonstrate to the most cynical of foreign critics that whatever else British politics might be they were strictly on the level.

First at a private meeting of the Pregnant with Meaning Society, later at a secret meeting of the

Carlton Club, the late Earl Baldwin expressed this truth in telling fashion when he said 'We are all Socialists now'. It was on this latter occasion that a leading member of the Club, excited by the aphorism, remarked to the late Lord Balfour 'That man Stanley B knows a thing or two'. To this Lord Balfour is alleged to have replied 'Even were we optimistic enough to assume the higher total to be correct, we might yet venture to doubt the ultimate adequacy of this sum of knowledge'.

Mr. Balfour in 1903. A contemporary caricature.

Lord Balfour was, of course, a sceptic and, during his long life-time, did much to popularize English scepticism abroad. He said things in Chicago, during the launching of the debt for World War I, and later, in

Paris, where he was helping to launch World Peace I, which showed that, given proper study of consumer-needs and strict adherence to delivery schedules, England could still successfully compete with the most skilled sceptics of those two cities.

His 'approach attitude' (which, as Menace of the University of Memphis, Tennessee, has pointed out, was essentially 'inner-directed') may have been influenced by his inability to see what was going to happen next. It was, however, an inability which he shared with Cobden. Both had unhappy experiences connected with the State of Illinois, though in other respects they were dissimilar. Thus Carlyle described Cobden as an 'inspired bagman'.

The question has often been asked: If it must be assumed that the people of past epochs in our history did not know what these epochs were leading up to, what made them go on? How did men – and women too – who could not have foreseen the 1950's, find the inspiration to carry out their often arduous day-to-day tasks as Reeves, Waterbailiffs, Canterbury Pilgrims and the like?

To them, after all, Blackpool, Llandudno, Scarborough, and even, in the fullest sense of the term, Bournemouth, were but seaside resorts, often inaccessible to all but the most intrepid holiday-makers, since the roads were already quite inadequate to the country's needs, and infested by sturdy beggars produced by the Enclosures. It must, moreover, be recalled that at that time any form of sea-coast was repellent to most

English folk, who mentally word-associated the sea around them with the bad fish which Protestant Elizabeth, no less than Roman Catholic Mary, compelled them to eat on Fridays. The fishing industry was feather-bedded.

Yet, with characteristic English pertinacity, they fared onward, buoyed up by a rugged faith that somewhere ahead lay, though still shrouded in obscurity, the twentieth century. It was the same spirit in which the late Earl Baldwin is reported to have said that, in moments of near-despair, he comforted himself with the thought that 'today' is only a prelude to the situation as it will be five hundred years hence.

Achievement of a just estimate of the past is doubly fraught with difficulty when we consider the entire question of economics. Modern man, with economics at his disposal night and day in every room of the house, finds it an almost impossible feat of the imagination to cast his mind back to a period when such amenities were virtually unknown. Not even the richest merchants of Tudor times had blue-prints.

It is true to say that in those days people in, for example, the upper Baron brackets, who could afford economics at all, tended to take them for granted. Others simply did without, doggedly performing yeoman service.

Lacking the aid of economics, many took refuge in religion, or service in foreign wars. Fighting to extend the wool trade or the slave trade, a healthy man could get as much economics as he wanted. Moreover, there were always institutions such as Venice and the Hanseatic League ready to supply lavish economics to Englishmen with characteristic stoutness of heart, character and so on. Anyone with a reasonably good S.H. rating could get into the Muscovy fur-trade and have economics on a scale which his grandfather, who might have been no more than a villein, would have envied.

A striking feature of the subsequent era was the fact that people were influenced – often publicly – by economists. Folk, that is to say, not only read what they wrote, but frequently acted on the assumption that it was true.

The early economists made their name by favouring *laissez-faire*. It was said of Adam Smith by a late eighteenth-century wit that, had he not existed, it would have been necessary to invent him. (The conception was, as is now known, far-fetched. He did exist, therefore it was not necessary to invent him.)

Although a Scotsman, and a contemporary, let us note, of Hume, A. Smith was in many ways a typical economist, and there were not wanting those who detected in his behaviour ominous warnings of things to come. He was hospitable, generous and jolly, but as early as Chapter XI of *The Wealth of Nations* he was going about London peering at girls in the streets, trying to make up his mind whether the English ones had better complexions than the Irish. This was a rash proceeding for a man in his position as Father of Political Economy, although it should be remembered that Sir

Robert Peel had not yet organized our modern police force.

There was worse to come, for, on deciding that the Irish were better looking, Smith gave wide publicity to the theory that this was the result of a potato diet. The deluded Irish, always apt to attach undue importance to personal appearance, immediately ploughed up everything else and planted potatoes, the result being the disastrous famine of 1847. The economist became known as Ould Ireland's Ruin, and – as Thackeray found when he visited the island – the names 'Smith' and 'Adam' are less common in Ireland than elsewhere.

Smith and his successors have been criticized on other grounds for 'wasting time'. Had they realized that *laissez-faire* and the Manchester School and so on were going to come to what Threat, of the University of Omaha, has described as 'a darned sticky end', would they not have been better advised to have let the Mercantile School peter out in the ordinary course of events and then move up fast as the twentieth century went into the straight? But they were essentially men of the Age, and we must remember that even *laissez-faire* seemed a good idea at the time.

To their credit be it said, however, that there were numerous economists of the period who, realizing they were all on the wrong tack, resolutely refused to write, or even think, about the subject. That is the sole reason why their names are now unknown.

It is scarcely possible to state the exact moment when economists began to decline in importance and influence. Before the first decade of the twentieth century was out, we find W. Hewins, ex-director of the London School of Economics, complaining with shrill bitterness of 'the indifference of statesmen, officials and business men, and the incapacity of the public to understand'. Maynard Keynes probably accelerated the process. His ideas were found to be a strain on the public mind, being perplexing when right and disastrous when wrong. There was approval for M. Norman, late Governor of the Bank of England, who said of Keynes's monetary theories 'there is no problem about money, except who has it'.

Norman was, of course, a sceptic, and his policy of lending freely to the Germans any English money that was not nailed down did much to encourage scepticism in others.

In Russia, economists picked their way gingerly among the deviations, 'always', as the whimiscal Radek had once put it, 'hoping against hope to achieve full Marx'. The Americans, restless as ever, were ceaselessly expanding the frontiers of the Harvard Business School and, eyes shadowed against the westering sun as it sank behind the high Sierras, were out looking for trends. Some 'struck it rich' and built themselves baroque mansions on Baruch Boulevard.

Others never came back, and maybe the sewers of Los Angeles could tell a tale.

But in England, though the economists' house organ *The Economist* fought on gallantly in their interests, and performers like Jay and Balogh and others still had their 'fans' who were sometimes responsible for hysterical scenes in the lecture halls of London or Oxford, more and more people were tending to handle economics on a do-it-yourself basis. Tax-evasion kits, and easy-to-make wage demands were becoming simplified.

In the pregnant words of the Chairman of General Directorates, England had 'called in the expense account to redress the balance of the account book'.

IV

COBURG FOR CHRISTMAS

It says here 'parthenogenesis'

THERE IS A SAYING current among the Lancashire peasantry which may roughly be translated as 'he who does not find a starting point will not proceed prosperously'.

In this sense, the first modern Englishman, Albert the Prince Consort, may well serve as a starting point for a more general summation of events. Some of these, we shall inevitably find, are as far apart as the early Christians, the early Victorians and the late War. Others are closer together.

Earlier and later events will be dealt with in subsequent chapters.

The method has, technologically, its disadvantages. To borrow the words of Lord Liverpool when he heard of the first railway locomotive, 'If it doesn't work, I suppose they'll try something else. If it does, it may be bye-bye to gee-gee'.

(He was no doubt embittered at the time by the fact that the only thing known about his policy as Premier was that it failed. He may also have recalled, with a certain nostalgia, what James I had done to improve British horse-breeding. He could hardly have foreseen the full development of the English reply to the French challenge at Newmarket in the late 1950's. But this is to anticipate.)

Like many Englishmen of his parentage and up-bringing, the second son of the Duke of Saxe-Coburg-Saalfeld was a German. Indeed numerous Germans at that time regarded their status as a matter of course, some even taking a modest pride in it. And the 'man behind-the-scenes' everywhere at the time was Baron Stockmar, another Coburg man.

As was the fashion of those days, cabals were formed, Lords Aberdeen, Palmerston and John Russell were seen everywhere, and thinking men were weighing the consequences, for good or ill, of the introduction of the penny postage.

Undeterred, the Prince Consort quietly perfected his plans for the improvement of Christmas.

The idea is said to have originated when the Prince chanced to overhear Baron Stockmar remarking to Baroness Lehzen that 'if a man makes a better Christmas, the world will tread a path to his door'. The Prince saw at once that fir trees and other Christmas kit of the German type were almost as easy-to-get in England as in the environs of Coburg. By the very early sixties, Messrs. Goodall of London, who previously had devoted themselves to the manufacture of playing-cards, had issued the first Christmas cards, with holly, robins, etc., designed by John Leighton.

'It comes', Baron Stockmar had commented some time earlier, 'but once (*bloss einmal*) a year', and the

COBURG FOR CHRISTMAS

Prince could not but assent. The Shop Early Movement had begun.

Nevertheless, as so often happens in our western democracies, the situation was not without its dangers. It was, in fact, no time for complacency. To subordinate the national well-being to sectional interests was the sheerest folly. What was required was above all unity of purpose, otherwise our moral leadership would inevitably be lost. The difference between freedom and licence was clear to everyone except to certain 'other-directional pattern groups' such as those great landowners who seemed, as one commentator puts it, 'to think they were living in the Middle Ages', to those factory-owners, all hard-faced and many tight-fisted as well, who seemed to think they could live on child labour, and to the Chartists, who seemed to think they were living in early 1918.

The period saw, too, a significant renewal of activity and influence on the part of the Foreign Extremists' and Agitators' Association which, since the days when Blake was arrested as a Napoleonic agent, had been more or less in eclipse. But, in a letter written in 1851, the Prince noted that opponents of his Great Exhibition were stating that members of the Association, gathering in Hyde Park for the occasion, were about 'to commence a thorough revolution here, to murder Victoria and myself, and to proclaim the Red Republic in England'.

In the event, the Association showed itself incapable of fulfilling any of these expectations. Its membership fell off sharply and it suffered a slow decline until revived by Sir William Joynson-Hicks and others in the 1920's.

It was a time of profound disillusionment. Many young people looked back with a puzzled envy to the 1830's. The Treaty of Nanking, ending the war with China, and the repeal of the Corn Laws had failed to satisfy the deeper needs of human nature. We, in our truer perspective, can see that they could not have been expected to do so. But to them it had seemed otherwise. Cholera had broken out in London, and over all hung the ever-increasing menace of the Railway. Other nations besides England were pressing ahead with its development, and people asked themselves whether civilization as they knew it was not doomed to extinction; whether in fact man had not, in the steam locomotive, evolved the instrument of his own destruction.

Small wonder that there were some only too ready to accept the crude and violent policies of Colonel Sibthorp as the 'way forward'. His prayer that either hail or 'a visitation of lightning' – his offer of an alternative evinced a certain political cunning – might destroy the roof of the Crystal Palace found open or tacit support in many unexpected quarters.

However, wiser counsels prevailed, and at the meeting of the British Association at Ipswich on 3rd July, 1851, the Prince was able to hear a paper read by Colonel Reid 'On Mooring Ships in Revolving Gales'. Immediately it was over another paper was read 'On the Contraction of Calico as shown in the Great Exhibition'. To the keen-sighted, the episode clearly indicated that the Early Victorians were inevitably giving place to the Mid.

By 1st August the Prince was at Osborne 'reading Radowitz's new *Gespraeche aus der Gegenwart*, which I like much for its just portrayal of parties and their views. What he is driving at, however, I cannot tell. I have also read a treatise by Owen on Parthenogenesis'.

This was an instance of early Group-Identification (which Kritz, of the University of Oklahoma, called 'Herd-Together-Feel'), and as such is of great significance. All up and down the country the New Middle Classes were reading Owen on Parthenogenesis and Radowitz's *Gespraeche*. They, too, could not tell what was being driven at.

It is in this sense that Radowitz has been hailed as 'the first Logical Positivist'.

The late Lord Balfour is reported to have said, in his inimitable manner, that 'history is an alternation between the steady, if stertorous, breathing of the drugged sleeper, and a series of hiccoughs often ending in strangulation'. Thus the period of general peace inaugurated in 1851 was marked by an almost unbroken succession of international conflicts of ever increasing ferocity and destructiveness.

The Prince may well have taken to heart the words attributed to Baron Stockmar on his death-bed, 'You ain't seen nothing yet'.

Fortunately, perhaps, he could not know that within less than fifty years of the withdrawal of the Sunday Trading Bill and the passing of the Jewish Disabilities

Bill there was going to be a *fin de siècle*, surely an unsuitable conclusion to the Victorian Age.

The succeeding years were a period of profound disillusionment. In their confusion and lack of direction, many young people found that, having learned to know all about Art, they had no idea of what they liked. The Boxer Rising, starting a short war with China, and some projected changes in the Betting Laws, failed to satisfy the deeper needs of human nature. And over all hung the ever-increasing menace of the motor-car. People asked themselves whether civilization as they knew it was not doomed to extinction. Had man evolved, in the horseless carriage, the instrument of his own destruction?

Small wonder that religion, traditional morality, sex, and standards of decency in public life were threatened with collapse, or that Youth, watching the puny efforts of its elders to save the situation by ordering car-owners to employ men with flags to walk in front of them, felt itself betrayed and plunged into cynicism, or rallied to the crude policies of Sir Henry Campbell-Bannerman.

V

DUMB

Or even friends?

MANY ENGLISHMEN have argued, and forcefully so, that a good deal that went, from time to time, wrong was basically due to mammals stopping being birds. And it is generally admitted that the turning point, the point, as some term it, of no return, was reached with serpents. The average Englishman has never been attracted by serpents.

Had it been possible to stop things at birds, toothless, and employing small stones in the gizzard to fulfil the digestive functions, it is clear that widespread results might have been avoided. Furthermore, convenient flight would have been continued without interruption and, as a bird-watching Member of Parliament said shortly after Blériot flew the Channel, 'all this expense could have been avoided by the exercise of a little foresight'.

The Minister replied that he would 'look into the matter', whereupon in a supplementary question a Member asked whether he 'proposed to revive the ancient custom of studying the entrails of birds to ascertain the auspices'. (Laughter.) Amid renewed laughter a member was understood to say that there were 'birds and birds'. (Laughter.) Amid general laughter, the Minister, 'laughing' as a Member, who afterwards withdrew his remark, said 'like a fool', said he 'rather thought not. We must see what happens'.

It was in a rare spirit of compromise that the early Englishman, grasping that a directional mistake had almost certainly been made somewhere and that it would have been better for all, including bears, to stay birds, faced the task of adjusting himself to his fellow mammals, many of whom were evidently planning on inhabiting the island for the duration. This early Englishman is described by C. E. Vulliamy, esteemed archaeologist, as having an 'enormously' thick neck. (It is a pity that he does not give us at any point a standard neck measurement by which to estimate his estimate of 'enormous'. The omission gives rise to the suspicion that Vulliamy may here be, to some extent, though doubtless not to any enormous one, the victim of what has become known as 'sensationalism'.)

'His cheekbones', remarks Vulliamy, who evidently knew the man well, 'were flat, but his prominent muzzle, and the *complete*' (italics mine) 'absence of a chin, gave him a brutish and sinister appearance. He walked with a shuffling gait, and was unable to assume a perfectly erect position'.

It is, unfortunately, impossible to comment at any length on this passage since it is understood to be subject to the *sub-judice* regulations, a number of men in trains, leading Generals, Trade Union Leaders, Editors,

Church dignitaries and others having lately instituted actions for libel on the ground that they are clearly recognizable and that the purpose of the description was to bring them into hatred, ridicule and contempt.

It will be recalled that the late Lord Balfour, on being asked by a friend for his advice as to whether to bring a libel action on these grounds or not, replied: 'The operative phrase is, of course, "*brought into* hatred, ridicule etcetera". What makes you think you were brought there instead of having been there, if you take my meaning, all the time?' None laughed more heartily at the sally than Lord Balfour's friend.

It is rather insufficiently realized to what extent wolves worried Englishmen throughout the centuries. Russians, who take wolves for granted, have scoffed – Catherine the Great it will be recalled, did so publicly – but the fact is that the people of Dulwich and the people of Tring – all of whom had experienced wolves – felt very badly about the matter. A wolf is not an English-type of hazard. It should be in a book.

A hitherto little-known piece of dialogue between the poet Alexander Pope and an un-named interlocutor throws some light on the English 'wolf-feel'.

Unknown Interlocutor: Pope, speaking as a well known poet, what seems to be your purely general reaction to wolves?

Alexander Pope: – Wolves?

U.I.: That's what I thought I said I said. Ha-ha.

A.P.: Same like spiders. Anti.

U.I.: Ha-ha-ha. The Scotsmen would hardly agree with you there, would they? I mean to say Bruce, what?

A.P.: I thought we were talking about wolves.

U.I.: Absolutely. Same thing really. Now here's where the *Annual Register* for this year says a wolf came down like – mind you this is what I'd call a bit of hyperbole myself – an Assyrian on the fold. Care to answer yes or no to that?

A.P.: A wolf in sheep's clothing would smell as sweet.

U.I.: Well thanks a lot, Alex. I can see you're going to be quite a controversial figure as the years flit by.

The truth, which only came to light after a good deal of investigation, was that while wolves are not a very great deal worse than anything else – there are, for instance, ants which can make wolves seem nearly cosy – the English got a fixation on wolves. And this for an obvious reason, namely, that wolves were the thing the English *got rid of.* Nobody knows the precise date on which the last wolf howled its last on English soil, but there is little doubt that there are no wolves now.

This makes all the difference between the life of the peasant in, for example, the northern foothills of the Carpathians and his 'opposite number' in the Southern foothills of, for instance, the Chiltern Hills. The difference in attitude, more specifically in the varying incidence of '*wolf-angst*' became, throughout the centuries, increasingly important, though much of this was, of course, in inverse ratio.

A particularly interesting aspect of Anglo-animal relationship over the centuries is the ox position. It would strain the limits of this study too far to deal with it in detail. Suffice it to say that at one time the English used oxen for drawing the plough (a comparatively primitive instrument at the period) and for pulling vehicles on the comparatively primitive roads. Later they used them less. Later still they did not use them for these purposes at all. The reason for these changes is unknown. The ox, however, while losing practical significance, on the whole gained in symbolic value, with an effect on religious thought resulting from the fact of the ox being listed by Moses along with neighbours' wives, manservants and maidservants as something not to be coveted. For a contemporary of Henry I not to covet an ox was a spiritually testing undertaking. By the time of Edward VII there was little disposition to do so, and many people found observation of at least a part of the Tenth Commandment that much easier. It was a factor which played its role in arresting the fall-off in Church attendance.

Sheep were esteemed, particularly as the prosperity caused by them in East Anglia led to the construction of churches which today seem to many absurdly disproportionate to the size of the local populations, and the need to find new markets for their wool inspired Englishmen to activities, such as the battles of Crécy and Agincourt, which might otherwise have been postponed or 'shelved' altogether. That is why at that period the term 'woolly thinking' was a high compliment, implying that the thinker concerned was either busy with a plan to raise the price of wool, or a scheme for conquering a section of north-western Europe. It has been noted as an example of the steady continuity of English outlook that this type of thinking continued to be widely employed long after its original motivations had become obsolete.

'Wool-gathering', the late Earl Baldwin is reported to have said, 'is a privilege of the English, and where should we have been without it?'

The late Ernest Bevin was, according to a man who saw him, even more outspoken. 'Show me', he cried, 'the man who does not gather wool and I will show you a long-haired intellectual'.

Suiting the action to the word, he unlocked a cupboard marked Top Secret and disclosed, to the keen gaze of his interlocutor, a long-haired intellectual. It must of course be admitted that Ernest Bevin was exceptional, in the sense that no other Englishman of his period was so typical as he. 'He stands together in the sense that he stands apart,' remarked the late Sir Stafford Cripps, adding, with a characteristic touch so characteristic of the essential man, 'so put that in your bloody pipe and smoke it'. A suffragan Bishop unreservedly agreed.

Following vicissitudes which, in the words of Sir Henry Campbell-Bannerman, 'hardened the nation's character like tempered steel, it seems to me', the horse and dog forced themselves successively into prominence. The theory that the English wanted horses – had, in other words, what is now called 'horse-compulsiveness' – is unsupported by evidence. Rather to the contrary, Henry VIII, whose whole attitude was essentially English, organized a mass massacre of horses compared to which nothing comparable in firmness and vigour of action was seen until it was realized that – given the animal-loving and basically kindly character of the population – the proper thing to do was to infect rabbits with a poisonous disease which will cause them to swell up and die in agony. Apart from its progressive and scientific quality, this type of action was discovered to be susceptible of saving farmers money and so, in our own day, British agriculture took a new step forward.

What Henry VIII faced was the fact of the existence of a large number of what he considered to be undersized horses. What he considered a full-sized horse was one capable of carrying a big man in full armour at a fast trot. In a boldly imaginative stroke, he issued, in 1546, an order that all horses failing to come up to Government specifications were to be killed off. Asked whether he thought that was a kind and nice thing to do, he replied that he had the assurance of his scientific horse-advisers that the action was essential in the national interest.

The massacre was almost wholly successful, and it was not until more than fifty years later that the Government realized that what was officially described as 'an error of judgment' had been committed. What, actually, were needed, were less big horses and more small ones. And there were men in Symrna ready to lay the foundations of the English thoroughbred horse.

They sold one to James I, and almost immediately the Duke of Newcastle went on record with the statement that what the monarch had been sold was, in the figurative sense of the word, a 'pup'.

The Duke was, as he had often been before, wrong. And the King, a new type of typical Englishman in the sense that he was a Scot, while trying to concentrate on the problem, experienced a flicker before the eyes on account of the Duke of Buckingham, of whose first encounter with the royal northerner Lord Clarendon remarked in his inimitable way that 'things have come to a pretty pass'.

However, though the Duke soon became murdered by a man who first pasted his name and address in his hat and then left it behind at the scene of the occurrence, horses went ahead, getting on the whole faster as time went on, but collectively rather than relatively faster, so that the position of men seeking to estimate the odds did not improve, and led to the gang-fights at Brighton which have already been mentioned as helping to bring English racing to its present position.

It was left to the dog – raggedly supported by the stag and the better sort of squirrel – to pull the English you-me-animal feel together. The attempt, made under the auspices of the Duke of F . . . to get squirrels *and* dogs injected with a painful poison which would cause them to swell up and die in agony, failed. The Duke, a leading land owner, in fact, swelled up and died in political agony. While regret was expressed in some quarters, it was realized that, in consequence, farmers were probably a shade better off. It was, as a former Bishop of London once said, 'just one of those goddamn things'. The Duke agreed that he had 'vastly enjoyed' the whole affair.

The English, it seems nearly certain, were from very early days aware of what the dog had done to the Abyssinians. For reasons which would split (as Bishop Berkely said in a dilemma much of which was of his own making, due to a fundamental misunderstanding of the nature and purpose of neo-philosophical techniques) 'something a good deal more solid than those Copts', the Abyssinians had first welcomed, then worshipped the dog.

They went so far as to elect a dog as their Prime Minister, and it is recorded that when the dog smiled at a Cabinet Minister it was taken as a sign that the favoured man should be elevated from the Home Office, where he was getting nowhere except into a morass of unpopularity due to the Abyssinian feeling about capital punishment (they liked it, but liked it to be done in such a way that it went on for a good long time, leaving opportunity for spectator sport), and seconded to the CID, known locally as 'the Copts'.

A person who got barked at by this dog was more or less definitely out.

Well appraised of the lessons of history, the English refused to elect a dog to the premiership, and when challenged with having so done were able to prove that the entity in question came well within the accepted legal definition of 'human being'.

During the mid-twentieth century, a sinister underground propaganda sought to spread, particularly among the more right-thinking peoples, the idea that Hitler had been fond of dogs, and thus should be excused. Dogs were quick to resent the imputation, and a Committee of Enquiry – though not particulary quick – was not slow, either, to establish that on the advice of Herr von Ribbentrop, who had reported that

'Crufts is England and England is Crufts *über Alles*', Hitler had taken a course of dog-love-pretence.

It must rank among the most serious criticisms of the late Sir Nevile Henderson, at that time English Ambassador in Berlin, that although he must have seen Hitler actually kick a dog, and on another occasion give an ill-natured caricature of a dog saying 'bow-wow', Sir Nevile failed to report either fact to the London Government, with consequences which are known.

Stalin's attitude to animals was equivocal. In a discussion with Mr Harry Hopkins about camels – the question at issue being the difference, if any, between the bactrian and the dromedary – Hopkins, after explaining the New Deal, remarked that the bactrian had, after all, only one hump. Stalin, who had been waiting with visible impatience to come in on cue with laugh-provoking statement, now said: 'And the dromedary, how many divisions has *he* got?'

On having the jest related to him, Edward VII remarked, with his usual foresight: 'But surely this belongs to future history?' And his embarrassed aide-de-camp was forced to admit that this was indeed the case.

FOOTNOTE

THERE'S GOOD in every century – if you'll only look for it. For those under the tremendous, and, it is hardly necessary to add, forward-pressing of English historical pressure, it will be desirable to offer at this point some guidance-notes on, in effect, how to interpret what went on and what to say about it when asked.

Questions, for instance, have been asked about the ultimate culture-status of the thirteenth century. The answer is that the thirteenth century had a placid love of the spiritual and showed it by enormous keenness in building cathedrals, many of them built below Trade Union rates, and without demarcation of demarcation lines.

Taken as a whole it failed to come off. The fourteenth century was on its tracks. About the fourteenth, it is otiose to say much except that while it was seeking on the one hand to fulfil the ideals of the thirteenth, it was nevertheless only too well aware of the stirrings which any time now were going to produce the fifteenth, a century – some people would not even dignify it with the name and described it as 'a tenner of decades' –

which attached itself to the sixteenth (virtually, one understands, walked into history on its arm with no questions about gate-crashers asked).

It is often asked whether the prestige enjoyed by the late sixteenth century is not, in essence, due to the effulgence of the early seventeenth century, and the true answer may well be that time will tell. The fact that it has not told so far is a point, but a blunt one. It was, however, as Hakluyt's voyages show, a time when a large number of people found 'something to write home about' and did. Muscovy was in the news.

From a strictly English point of view, the eighteenth century was not so much a mistake as an error in judgment. If people had been on the lookout a bit more smartly, it might never have come to pass. Yet, and it is a notable tribute to the English genius, no sooner had the islanders found themselves addled with Pope, Johnson and other habitués of the period, than they arranged to accept them on what was known at the time as 'a genius basis'. A man, in other words, who claimed to get in on the eighteenth century, had to guarantee genius or money refunded. The number of repossessions was surprisingly low. Garrick had a little trouble, but this proved to be due to a misunderstanding about something he thought Boswell thought he had heard Garrick say he thought.

The nineteenth century requires no recommendation from us, and the twentieth is what we have here on the left as we leave the building. The iron work is by Krupp.

The Enquiry Bureau has also had to deal with many

enquiries as to the degree to which the English are 'good' tempered, or – on the other hand, and the existence of this dubiety has caused a good deal of trouble to some – 'bad' tempered. A Frenchman whose name, though on record, is unimportant, said in sixteen something that the English were, above all things, cheery, kind, gay, and loved fine food. They drank, with enjoyment, but with a proper restraint induced by the realization that alcoholic excess is, ultimately, a deterrent to a full appreciation of The Grape, a lot. Yet, and it is the task of the historian to know why, continentals were accusing Englishmen of the 'spleen'. (A Corsican Leader who knew Boswell said he thought it was alcoholic poisoning, but he would like a second opinion. He knew the English had a way of their own with that type of thing. 'I've always said', said he, 'your poultices are wonderful'.)

And so as the sun rose over Eccleston Square, germ of Transport House to be, people – not without regret – said 'goodbye' to the eighteenth century. It had, after all, been worth while.

VI

THE FABRIC

William Blake - the man

CONTINUITY in diversity and, to a considerable extent, *vice versa*, have always been salient characteristics of English social and political life, and had, a contemporary of Henry II been able to revisit London in Chaucer's day, it is safe to say that he would have found many changes to note.

True, housewives still ascended to upper windows in the traditional way to empty their slops on the head of what was still called 'the unwary pedestrian', just as they had on the day the knights rode by on the way to Canterbury and their controversial interview with Thomas à Becket. But already the Age of Jostle had begun. In the narrow streets, apprentices jostled pages in their multi-coloured doublets, friars jostled summoners, and the pack-horses of merchants deliberately jostled bearded mariners with many a tale to tell of argosies (as fleets or convoys were then termed). The historical novel was virtually on the way.

Our time-traveller would have found that the Isle of Dogs, which in his day had been so-called by a corruption of the term 'Isle of Ducks', a name it had acquired earlier because of the quantity of the fowl which used to gather there, now housed the greyhound kennels of Edward III. The English dog had begun to come into his own, though he still had a long way to go.

Only a few hundred years later, with England the greatest maritime power, etymologists could argue with some force that the name had all along been a corruption of the phrase 'Isle of Docks', which was what the area had all along been going to become. The point is that it was the same island – as the egregious Goering was soon to find to his cost when he loosed the notorious *Luftwaffe* on East London.

Confused by the characteristic English blend of traditionalism and innovation, an inquiring Soviet diplomat once asked the late Ernest Bevin, then Foreign Secretary, why there were still Tories in England nowadays, but, apparently, no Whigs. Ignorant of English democratic ways, the diplomat all too evidently suspected that the Whigs had been either massacred during the Labour Party's long struggle for power, or transplanted *en masse* to the grim settlements of Caithness and Sutherland.

The Foreign Secretary was able to assure him, in his blunt fashion, that so far from any *ukase* against Whigs having been issued, freedom for Whiggery was implicitly guaranteed by the Constitution. 'In our modern State they may not always care to parade their views,' said Mr Bevin, 'but I could take you to clubs crowded with them. Nor, if they behave themselves, are they in any danger from the police. Within certain limits, Whiggery is not incompatible even with membership of the Party, and many Whigs who are prepared to co-operate frankly and honestly with us, hold positions of trust and influence today.'

The diplomat, visibly impressed, said that he would certainly convey these assurances to Moscow where they would be received with relief and would do much to further the cause of Anglo-Soviet friendship.

(In this connection, the question is often asked: What would Ernest Bevin have done had he been Foreign Secretary at the time of the annexation – or as some prefer to call it 'Revestment' – of the Isle of Man by the English Parliament in 1763? The question is a valid one. A distinguished Labour Party historian has given it as his view that the Labour Party would have avoided the high-handed and provocative actions of undemocratically minded officers of Revenue and Excise which embittered our relations with the Man people for years. On the other hand, it certainly would not have countenanced the lawless and unconstitutional activities of a clique of professional smugglers, seeking to mask their true aims in the guise of an out-moded Manx nationalism. The same, *mutatis! mutandis!*, can probably be said of Ireland.)

Like a golden thread through English history runs the English spirit of compromise, the realization that you cannot have one thing without another. It would have been un-English to have carried on the struggle for the maintenance of established law and the sanctity of commercial contracts against the menacing forces of France at the end of the eighteenth century without repeatedly suspending the Habeas Corpus Act and also cash payments by the Bank of England.

In the same way, the era of gross material prosperity and well-being embarked upon some years later was mitigated by the commercial panic of 1825-6, the commercial panic of 1846, the commercial panic of 1857 and the suspension of the Bank Charter Act, the commercial panic of 1866, the devastating outbreak of foot and mouth disease in 1870, the coal-famine of 1873, the great depression of 1878, the destructive hurricane of 1881, the awful drought of 1886, the deadly influenza epidemic of 1890, and the Boer War.

It has been a profound awareness of this spirit of compromise which has enabled Englishmen throughout the ages to make assertions and predictions which might otherwise be considered rash.

Blake set a notable example with his announcement that he would not 'cease from mental fight, nor shall the sword sleep in my hand' until we had – as he phrased it in his slightly extravagant way – 'built Jerusalem in England's green and pleasant land'.

He must certainly have been aware – and if he was not, he was guilty of a frivolous disregard of facts of which H.M. Government were only too vividly conscious, and might justifiably incur the charge of irresponsible demagoguery – that prevailing conditions precluded the hope that his programme could be carried out in the near, or even in the more distant, future. The materials were simply not available.

In such circumstances, to call for a permanent state of mental fight was, as the Home Secretary said at the time, to 'demand the impossible'.

It must be said, however, in fairness to Blake, that it is far more probable that he had never intended his remarks to be treated as a rigid blueprint for immediate action, but rather as the broad sketch of a general line of policy to be followed in so far as was compatible with changing conditions and the demands which might be made upon our resources for other purposes.

In this sensible and thoroughly practical approach to the problems of the day, he was imitated by many successors who felt able to announce their categorical refusal to sheath the sword until something probably unattainable had been attained, to shake hands with murder, to leave or return to the Gold Standard, to betray our loyal Jewish and/or Arab friends and Allies, without whose sacrifice in the cause of freedom the fabric of civilization as we know it might well have crumbled beneath the blows of the aggressor, to forget the gallant officers and men of our incomparable Army when the War and the national peril are a thing of the past and they are faced with old age and possible penury.

It is an aspect of English life which has won the admiration of foreign observers that what may be termed 'the Blake approach' has been common to all parties, none of them seeking to take a mean advantage or steal a march on others by a fanatical consistency.

For the benefit of those to whom the name of 'Blake' may appear as something of a bizarre novelty, it may be added that in addition to writing and drawing – both of these being activities likely to keep his mind reasonably fit – he walked about London wearing a red knitted French 'Liberty' cap, showing sympathy with the oppressed, though not with the excesses which they later committed. Another point about him was that while living on the South Coast – in, not to put too fine a point upon it, Sussex – he employed, as what was later termed a 'jobbing gardener', an ill-tempered soldier who, on being told to 'get on with the cauliflowers or get back to whatever battlefield you conceive to be open to you', took exception, and an action for assault.

The poet Blake, twisting the man's arms behind his back, then invented the 'knee-hack' and took the discomfited warrior back to his billet. Despite heavy pressure of other news, the *cause* became *celèbre*.

VII

GROWING PAINS

Lenin 'misses the bus'

THE ENGLISH PEOPLE being, like other 'peoples', essentially 'peace-loving', there has inevitably been controversy regarding the role of 'war' in their history. There can be little doubt that at one time civilian historians, fascinated by diagrams, with squares and small flags, showing what went wrong at the battles of Cannae, Fontenoy, etc., and their judgment warped by an inferiority complex *vis-à-vis* Clausewitz, paid far too much attention to this kind of thing.

After all, as has been well said, making due allowance for certain differences in the type of weapons in use at different periods, and recognizing that the question 'Who won?' is always of some interest, one battle is very much like another. With similar qualifications, the same may be said of conflicts at sea.

Later, as Economics (see passim) became more widespread, it began to be felt that Clausewitz was both cynical and German, as was shown in the remark he made about politics, and many took the view that time and space could be saved by omitting battles, and even war *as such*, from history books altogether.

This, like so many moves in the right direction – one

may instance Darwin, the temperance movement in the United States, and the Russian revolution – went too far.

Though battles in themselves are rightly held to be both uneconomic and anti-social, wars can and sometimes do produce effects in the economic field which may justifiably be described as 'important', due account being, of course, taken of the fact that whatever happened would have happened any way in the long run, as a result of progress.

As Henry VI wrote in a private letter to Joan of Arc shortly before she paid the inevitable penalty for her rash, though doubtless sincere, course of action, 'much as we may all deplore some of the episodes of the last fifty years, and I would be the last to deny that there have been moments when all thoughtful men and women must have been gravely troubled, yet if these events have done something to bring about a better understanding of the character and aims of our two peoples, then the sacrifices we have all made will not have been in vain'.

It was said, privately, that Joan (as she was familiarly known) was much touched by this evidence of English goodwill.

Both Jack Cade, who, when all is said and done, did behead the acting head of the Treasury in 1450, and – stepping back a pace to earlier social conditions – Wat Tyler, who beheaded the Archbishop of Canterbury, held this optimistic view. Tyler, after being first tricked, then slain, said as he lay dying that he 'felt the class relationship had at least been clarified'.

He had, of course, failed to realize that English public opinion rarely sanctions the public execution of the Archbishop of Canterbury.

The position of the so-called Parliamentarians in the attitude they adopted towards Charles I is less immediately clear. There were many thinking men in the country who felt that if only Pym, Hampden, Cromwell and the like, had 'held their horses', and had realized that the sheer weight of enlightened public opinion was going to be brought to bear *by constitutional means*, they would have desisted from the actions which – as at Naseby – they subsequently took.

Had they so desisted, it seems unlikely that Charles II would have had any case at all.

On the other hand, it must be admitted that Cromwell, by teaching cavalry to fight in leather jerkins, did almost as much for the English horse as James I had done. The War Office was against it, and even in 1664 'Black Tom' General Lord Fairfax described what we should now call good horses as 'over-valued pygmy baubles'. He also did much to spread the notion that racing men were 'cissies'. It was not until the stern gang-fights of 1936 on Brighton racecourse that this imputation was finally refuted.

The truth probably is that, whereas the English were not always able to arrange for foreign wars to take the proper course, it was always in the power of Englishmen to avoid civil wars by – as later happened – bringing in democracy.

The conflict with Spain in the days of Frobisher and

many others of his kidney laid the foundations of the English Mercantile Marine. (A man who stated at the trial of Sir Walter Raleigh that he had been deluded into supposing that a mercantile marine was an officer of the Royal Marines operating on the Black Market was expelled from the Spanish Main and had his licence endorsed.)

What happened in between is too confused and controversial to be dealt with here. England 'gained' Canada. And the spice trade flourished.

And then England found itself face to face with Napoleon. Had Napoleon known, as the English did,

that the lust for power and naked aggression simply do not pay, Napoleon – who ended his life in relative indigence and obscurity on the island of St Helena – might, in the fullness of time, have done the same thing on his native island of Corsica without ever bothering to move himself from the Bonaparte family homestead.

All through the succeeding century the English were learning more and more about the nature and purpose of war. It has been said that the wars of the two hundred years preceding the period of about fifty years ago consolidated capitalism and led to imperialism, with the result that both Karl Marx and V. Lenin applied for tickets to the reading-room of the British Museum with the idea of finding out what was going on.

The charge has been made that had a different course been adopted, both of these – even allowing for the excitable Jewish temperament of the one and the Slavonic one of the other – would have been prepared to call it a day and join the Labour Party, to the mutual advantage of all concerned.

The view is superficial.

The Labour Party was already on the way.

There are those who claim that the Boer War caused the Labour Party. This is an exaggeration. What the Boer War caused was, in the first place, a certain amount of pacifism. As a distant relative of the Duke of B - - - shire wittily remarked at the time 'D - - n it, a fellow doesn't want to be mixed up in a Jameson Raid every day of the b - - - - y week'.

(This was the same relative who afterwards inspired the poem of the late Rudyard Kipling on the subject of the 'Duke's son, cook's son, son of a belted earl'. This has sometimes been interpreted as a panegyric of unbridled non-class-consciousness. The fact is that the duke's son was the father of the cook's son, who later was adopted as a result of the incidence of death duties on leading families, by an earl, for tax exemption purposes.)

The Boer War also gave rise to the phrase 'pro-Boer'. Hitherto, Englishmen had tended to be 'pro' this and 'anti' that without much thought of the consequences. 'We leave all that sort of thing to the Frenchies', as a relative of the Duke of C - - - shire wittily remarked when somebody asked him whether he would sit for a pro-tem prototype of an Anti.

When, however, English men and women of every class and condition saw the late Lloyd George leaving Birmingham Town Hall disguised as a policeman for fear of a mob which was seeking to lynch him as a pro-Boer, wiser counsels prevailed.

Thus by 1906 the Labour Party had thirty members of the House of Commons. But it was after the war of 1914-18 (which ended a halcyon period of English life in which, except for the railway strike, the coal strike and the general expection of imminent disaster, there was not a cloud in the sky), that the Labour Party and all that we mean by up-to-date Conservatism came into their own.

It is for this reason that it was known as the First *Great* War.

VIII

MOSCOW'S DOMES

Things kings can do

DESPITE DISPUTES a good feature of English history has always been the steady maintenance of relations. Anglo-Scottish, Anglo-Russian, Anglo-American, and – to draw attention to a facet of the situation which has been too often overlooked – Anglo-Irish relations have all played their due part in what a Chicago University Foundation Study has rightly termed 'the essential on-move of English on-the-wayness'. The Study, with a measure of justice, points out that if the English have not got on-move so fast as some others, there is probably a perfectly reasonable explanation.

It is unnecessary to go here, in any detail, into the case of Parnell. It is both familiar and confusing. Nor do several of the protagonists come well out of an affair which, for this very reason, is best left to what a leading bookmaker, chatting at Homburg in 1909 with Edward VII, wittily described as the 'stern arbitrament of the future'.

The monarch was much impressed by the aphorism and when the bookmaker was later fraudently charged with fraudulent practices said that he regretted that such a thing should have happened. It was a remark fully characteristic of his broad-minded *bonhomie* – fervently greeted in a France still smarting from the effects of the situation in North Africa as '*L'entente cordiale*'. Never did the Eiffel Tower stand closer to St Paul's Cathedral than on that day.

Edward, known as 'the peacemaker' on the ground that he averted a war with France in favour of a war with Germany – a sensible plan which had long engaged the attention of English planners who, nevertheless, had until then despaired of engaging a royal interest in their designs – was intelligibly amazed when the late Lord Balfour remarked to him one day in the course of a general discussion of the soul of man, that the thing to do was to 'nobble the Russkis. After all,' commented Balfour, having reference to Tzar Nicholas II, who was proposing to visit England in the guise of an Admiral, 'old Popeye the Sailor's some sort of cousin of yours isn't he? Or am I right?'

'First', responded the incumbent of the British throne.

'So go in and win', was the cheery admonition of one upon whose fundamental wisdom, however deeply coated from time to time with a top-layer of cynicism which (as Lord Balfour's butler admitted) from time to time 'fair gave you the sick', he was wont to rely.

The story is told of how the King, who until assuming that position had been Prince of Wales, at this point lowered his billiard cue, cancelled a pre-arranged bout at baccarat, and said to Balfour: 'Name Napea mean anything to you?'

The luckless Earl-to-be, at the time the merest Mr, acknowledged himself nonplussed. 'Doesn't seem to ring a bell at all', he said. 'Wonder', he suggested, 'if Secretary of State for War Haldane would know? Say what you will, he's a clever chap. Remember how we laughed when he said Germany was his spiritual home? His great-aunt was a friend of the Hegels. Naturally she was a mere slip of a girl at the time. And furthermore,' added the excited Balfour, who was nothing if not fair-minded, 'don't you run away with the idea Hegel knew anything about that Marx business. He'd never heard of the man. As for originating him, or being the philosophical source from which, and all that type of caper, forget it, Teddy, forget it. He hadn't a clue.'

'Arthur,' responded the ever-genial man-of-the-world who nevertheless harboured a very very deep and sincere understanding of what may be called, in an inevitably English understatement, Kingship, 'you got what we in Hanover used mostly always call the "*goldener Herz*". Is already good, but not to let it go soft on you. After all, are you boss of the Innenminister – what you call Home Secretary – or not? Keep a sense of proportion, hang it all!'

'Hanging them as fast as the police can pick them up', replied the Prime Minister surlily. In a rare outburst of temper he slashed with his billiard cue at a futuristic picture of the future Lord Northcliffe (then Mr Harmsworth) which hung upon the wall of the room like a thing, and cried: 'It's well enough for you, me merry monarch, with languages tripping naturally off yer tongue like as if the wee folk (Lord save us) had given ye the gift, but with me not having the Gaelic how are you imagining in that starry head of yours with the eyes on ye that stand out like it was closing time and you not noticing the clock till near the fatal moment, how d'you expect, me broth of a b'hoy, that I could, even under more favourable circumstances than those pertaining, have carried out, with more than a very slender modicum of success, my duties as Chief Secretary for Ireland in the year – if memory serves – 1887?'

'Spalpeen,' vouchsafed the other, ruminatively.

'Anything you say,' agreed the philosopher-statesman.

'Honestly,' said the best-beloved of Europe's rulers, 'I do find that a bit much. Anything I say? Have I been able for the last five minutes to get a word in edgeways? What, may I have the honour of asking, has happened to my story about Napea?'

'OK,' snapped the Man Who Put Thought On the Map, 'let's have it.'

It was thus that from the lips of Royalty itself he first heard the story of the beginning of Anglo-Russian relations, in the year 1556.

'It had,' said Edward, when he was satisfied that his cigar was "drawing properly", 'for some time been realised that Anglo-Russian relations were a "soft spot" on an otherwise satisfactory graph of what was later to be referred to with ever-increasing distaste, as the "international situation".

With a view to remedying this, a decision was taken

at top level to invite to London a man called Osep Napea, special envoy of the Tzar. After some hesitation in the Kremlin, the invitation was accepted, and Napea, loaded with costly gifts, set out in an English vessel to take his first look at what was currently known in Moscow as 'the western way of life'.

As a result, possibly, of sabotage, or else of a mere ordinary lack of appreciation of the importance of this situation to the nation, the meterological office gave categorical assurances that conditions in the North Sea (later to be described offensively by *provocateurs* as the 'German Ocean') were entirely favourable, with blue skies, nothing but blue skies all the day long. As Fate, ill-luck – call it what you will – would have it, a storm blew up of such a nature that the Captain could not refrain from remarking that it was rendering this his worst crossing for eleven months. To cut a long story short, the entire party was wrecked on the coast of Scotland, not, as a Russian security officer stated later, 'a hundred miles from Aberdeen.'

With the utmost difficulty Napea struggled ashore and sat down on a rock, feeling thankful. He was pleased, too, to see that the place was far from desolate – a big crowd of Scotsmen was hurrying to the beach. Now, he thought, everything would be all right, and he admired their courage and devotion as they dashed into the waves to salvage the goods. The next thing he saw was the same crowd disappearing at a fast rate into the hinterland, taking with them everything that could be moved, including all his clothes.

Hakluyt reports that 'the whole mass and body of the goods laden in the ship was by the rude and ravenous people of the Countrey thereunto adjoining, rifled, spoyled and carried away, to the manifest loss and utter destruction of all the lading of the said ship.' The English Government rushed some spare suits to Scotland and got the Ambassador to Edinburgh, but he kept saying: 'What about all those things I brought with me?' and goodwill was being fast dissipated.

The Queen's Commissioners assured him – they seem to have been scandalously lacking in expert knowledge of conditions pertaining in Scotland – that they would go up to the scene of the shipwreck with strict orders that all property was to be returned immediately, and they actually did issue a lot of proclamations and edicts, saying did people grasp that, if this sort of thing went on, the next thing there would be a Cold War?

'By reason whereof,' – of the Proclamations and Edicts, that is – 'not without great labours and pains and charges, after long time divers small parcels of wax and other small trifling things of no value were, by the poorer sort of the Scots, brought to the Commissioners, but the jewels, rich apparel, presents, gold, silver, costly furs and such like, were conveyed away, concealed, and utterly embezzled.'

The Ambassador waited in Edinburgh for days and days while the Scots 'by subtle and crafty dealings' so acted that 'no effectual restitution was made'. Finally he 'fatigated', and the whole party went off to London in a foul temper. They tried to cheer up the Russian by laying on a fox-hunt near Islington, but it took a long time for the harm to be undone.

'Like it, ? queried the titular chief of an Empire upon which at that time of epoch the sun never set.

'Good story,' assented the Premier. 'Any truth in it?'

'Listen, A.J.,' said the direct descendant of Queen Victoria, a touch of asperity now noticeable in his already rather mannered manner, 'I ought to tell you there's a story going the rounds that you're some kind of a cynic. Never believed it myself – rebutted it, in fact, with all the force at my command. But now . . . I . . . well, I wonder . . .'

However, as George Malcolm Young, C.B., M.A., has written, the opening of the twentieth century saw English society, growing less formal, 'irradiated with the wit and charm of the group known to themselves, and others, as "the souls". Balfour's lightness of touch, his fresh fancy, his airiness of manner never concealed from those who knew him an inner earnestness and depth of feeling'.

Knowing him well, King Edward, after a reflective pause, said: 'Your airiness of manner does not conceal from me an inner earnestness and depth of feeling.'

'Thanks very much,' replied Lord Balfour; 'what you momentarily mistook for "cynicism" was merely and simply part of my effort to enable George Malcolm Young to remark some time on the example I left "of the philosophic mind immersed in public business and never compromising its own integrity".'

'Fair enough.'

'Quite. But you were saying, Sire?'

'I was simply saying that the entire story of Ambassador Napea and the beginning of Anglo-relations is factually true and may be read in the pages of Hakluyt.'

'Good God!' commented the future author of the Palestine Declaration of 1917, so unhappily inconsonant with another declaration made by the same author in the same year, 'looks like a grey vista of the years, what?'

It was as a result of this episode that Lord Balfour, to the end of his days, regarded with a certain misgiving what was otherwise fairly well known as 'the Russian experiment'.

IX

BESIDE THE MILLPOND

Washington stands firm

THE AMERICANS, and what have been termed with more than a touch of the *insouciance* – associated in the unhistorically-conditioned mind with Calvin Coolidge and (to employ a period term) 'the boys' – Anglo-American relations, differed widely from Anglo-Russian relations. For reasons which can be readily understood by anyone who takes the trouble to glance at a geography book and some reliable calendar, Anglo-American relations came after Anglo-Russian relations.

It was sometimes difficult for Englishmen to explain this to members of the American Congress.

Senator Pewson, in a statement which later led to the establishment of a committee to investigate the Senate on the ground that if things went on like this almost anything might happen, asked why it was that the English had entered into relations with the Russians before doing so with the United States. A State Department expert, with geography book and calendar, sought to prove that the Russians had, in the broadest sense of the word, existed before the Americans. Charged, during the coffee-break, with an immoral offence against a minor, during the lunch break with high treason, and – over a very welcome cup of tea – with running a chain of brothels, gaming houses and/or Trade Unions in Miami, the official in question, whose name was given in one authentic account as 'Foggy Bottom' and in another as 'Striped Pants' excused himself on the ground that when he said 'Russians' he had meant 'Russians as such', more or less.

Senator Mewson then asked leave to read into the record the entire story of Anglo-American relations from then till now.

Leaping to his feet and asking if Senator Mewson would yield, Senator Chewson was gratified to hear from the lips of Senator Mewson: 'I yield 25 seconds of my time to the Senator'. (This being at the time the already mentioned Chewson.)

Courteously thanking, in what is known as 'fried boloney southern style', the Senator from some place in New England (this latter being none other than Mewson), Chewson, in a rapid but clear voice, then read a portion of the Second Book of Kings and a piece of advice on how to keep bees in a drought. An English member of Parliament who was present, but asked that his name be not mentioned – it was Ernle-Bailby-Ernle-Smith and he thought the effect on Anglo-American relations might be bad – said to Chewson: 'Mean to say you can get away with that?'

'Certainly,' riposted Chewson, 'you effete representative of a long out-of-date Empire . . .'

'Mind saying "Commonwealth",' EBES was audacious enough to interpose, 'just for the record?'

'Free franking, what you call mailing,' Chewson was understood to be saying, 'get that bee-stuff read into the Record and I've *gratis* told the voters about bees.'

'Jolly good show!' hazarded the Englishman, attempting an Americanism which he instinctively felt would win the approval of his genial host.

'Put it there, pardner,' hazarded the transoceanic statesman, attempting an anglicism which he instinctively felt would win the approval of his genial guest. 'Snafu, I kinda reckon, buddy,' he added, winning thereby a sycophantic pat from a stripe-panted cat at that time in charge of the women's section of the protocol section of the State Department section of that other-directing power-get-together known to journalists, too often, unfortunately, more interested in a sensational story than in the basic facts of the world today, as 'the American Government'.

Having gained the confidence of his American colleague and political *vis-à-vis*, the English exile, though his thoughts were all of a spring morn in Marylebone, with daffodils abloom where the sweet English earth rises toward St John's Wood, suggested, as a useful subject for discussion, the position and significance of President Monroe. 'The one, I mean,' he said, for fear of misunderstanding, 'with the Doctrine.'

'Such a discussion', replied the Senator, 'would be both a privilege and a pleasure. Personally I esteem Monroe. Any time you want to get his Doctrine pigeon-holed, give me – how you say, limey? – a blow on the buzzer.'

Reading from a prepared manuscript handed him the previous evening by the British Embassy, the English-Speaking Union and the Council for General Improvement, the cis-ocean legislator remarked that obviously any definitive reassessment of the role of the President in American Government – and never, surely, has such reassessment been more urgently required – must of necessity take as its starting-point James Monroe.

To begin with, he was quite certainly the *fifth* President. Furthermore, he was the immediate successor to James Madison. To this the American readily assented.

His Doctrine, resumed the Member of the Mother of Parliaments, is well known under the name of 'The Monroe Doctrine' and requires no comment.

'No comment,' nodded Chewson with evident relish. 'I like that. Give the newspapers an inch and they give you hell. It's', he expatiated, struck by the mystified look of the Englishman, 'a sort of play on words. Put it this way. There's an expression people use that says – don't ask me why, but there was probably some reason – "give them an inch and they'll take an ell".'

'Oh I say, awfully authentic actually,' cried the Sussex denizen. 'And may I take this opportunity to say, very very sincerely, that every time I revisit the United States I am more and more impressed by the widening of knowledge, the deepening of culture, the sense of centricity, other-mindedness, culture – if you follow me – and how the Rockefellers have changed since the old days when...'

'Good-o!' chuckled the US denizen. 'Proceed, I beg you, with your tale. I should enjoy it of all things. You interest me vastly.'

'Suffice it merely', said Ernle-B-Ernle-S, reading from his MS 'to remind the student for the sake of clarity' – here he stopped reading and spoke *extempore*, 'that in this connection the terms "Monroe" and "Doctrine" are incorrect and should not be used. The whole notion had been suggested to Monroe by somebody else, and the President did not mean it to be a Doctrine, but just a statement.'

(Schouler tells the story of how a well known Washington wag, hoping to 'get a rise' out of the incumbent of the White House, said to him with affected solemnity: 'Mr President, what was that Doctrine you came out with last night?' Quick as a flash came the reply: 'That was no Doctrine, that was my message to Congress.'

The tale, Ernle was careful to point out, may well be apocryphal, but well illustrates the President's reputation for dry wit.

John Quincy Adams did not, however, exaggerate when he remarked that it was Monroe's intention to point out to anyone who was interested that the Americas were 'occupied by contiguous states'. In other words, he wanted to explain that country A was next to B, and so on.

This he did, on 2nd December, 1823. And in the far off fog-shrouded city by the Thames, as *roués* and bucks foregathered at Almack's and Vauxhall Gardens, discussing the late Regency, Britain's George Canning unreservedly agreed.

A point had thus been reached in Anglo-American relations.

More important is the fact, mentioned by several biographers and never seriously questioned, that Monroe 'had deep-set eyes'. Though the first steamship had yet to sail from Bristol to New York, and many other developments due to occur some time had not yet occurred, the era of deep-set eyes, which was to leave so profound a mark upon American political life, had begun.

We have it, insisted Ernle, and the other could not deny the allegation, on the authority of Washington Irving that President Madison, who – we are on solid ground here – was the fourth President, and had thus assumed office many years after the all-important invention of the cotton-gin, with its effects on cotton, was 'wizened'. It can be taken for granted that had Madison had deep-set eyes, Irving would have mentioned them.

Abraham Lincoln had 'grey deep-set eyes' (Monroe's were 'greyish blue', but the main trend is unmistakable) and so did most of these men of unswerving character and vision who in those years were blazing the trail which led, as can be seen in the perspective of history, directly to subsequent events.

Abuses there were, certainly – notably the notorious 'Cedar Street Scandal' of 1887. Investigation eventually proved beyond a reasonable doubt that a man known to the underworld as 'Popeye the Sailor' – apparently in reference to his activities as a dope-peddler on the Hoboken Ferry – had, by systematic corruption of witnesses and falsification of photographs, risen to a position of trust in which millions passed daily through his hands.

To the last, several of his victims claimed they considered his eyes 'sort of deep set', and only the intervention of J. P. Morgan averted general panic. The prestige of the Republican Party in the 'key' States east and west of its traditional strong-hold suffered severely, and had not the prestige of the Democratic Party in the same areas suffered equally, political consequences might well have ensued.

Even so – and foreign critics may note this as an example of the inherent strength and resilience of American institutions – the Centenary of the adoption of the Federal Constitution was celebrated that year at Philadelphia with a procession five miles long, and Britain's Joseph Chamberlain was entertained at dinner by the New York City Chamber of Commerce.

'I for one', interpolated The Voice of Britain, 'have noted that. One isn't an M.P. for nothing. Shall I continue?' Suiting the action to the word, he remarked that for the country as a whole those were halcyon days. By 1900 the events of 1899 were already in the past, and the Panama Canal had not been dug. There must have been many a placid citizen who supposed that the situation had come to stay. Many had even forgotten that it was a situation at all.

But they, like so many others before and since, had under-estimated the essential dynamic of American life. And before the century was a year old, everything had changed.

Leon Czolgosz, who on 6th September, 1901, at Buffalo N.Y., shot and fatally wounded President McKinley, automatically elevating Theodore Roosevelt to the Presidency, not only drew attention to the Vice-Presidency and sowed the seeds of the Nixon controversy; he ended an epoch.

From now on the future belonged to men like Theodore Roosevelt himself (see full-face portrait left), Herbert Hoover (portrait opposite repays careful study), Dwight Eisenhower, and Adlai Stevenson (examine press photographs).

Even shrewd Calvin Coolidge, whose eyes when he was at his shrewdest were nearly invisible, never claimed that they were deep set. His hard-bitten New England background enabled him to judge immediately which way the wind was blowing. Cross-questioned by correspondents, he re-told his story about the preacher being opposed to sin, and then retired from public life.

'Have I said enough?' queried EBES, 'and by the way, Spewson,' he said, 'do call me Ebes. Saves time apart from anything else'.

'Not Spewson, Chewson,' that worthy felt bound to interject.

'Forget my own name next,' smiled the Sussexer, 'Not that anyone might not. Whatsay, Bluesome, if that's what you said?'

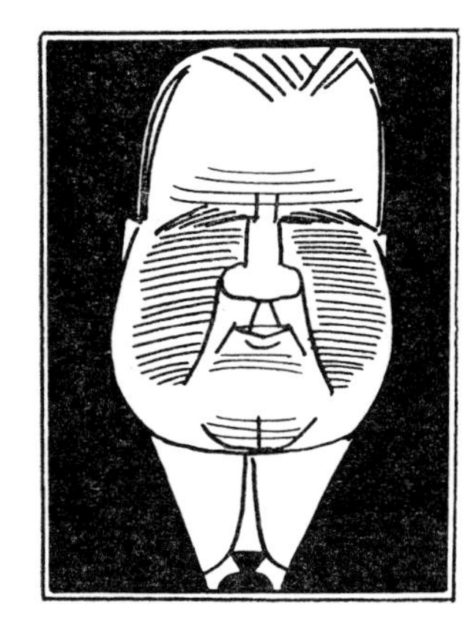

'As an American,' replied Chewson, 'I concede the right of any man to forget his own name, next, last or all the time. Yet, as I survey the storm clouds which threaten each and all of us with a catastrophe in which General Motors – nay, I will go further, and say even General Electric – cease to exist, when I consider, as it is my duty to do, the obligations which citizenship of a country extending, as it does (and I say so without fear of valid contradiction) from just immediately south of Canada to where it uninterruptedly becomes Mexico, impose upon me, be I Catholic, Presbyterian, Buddhist or Jew, I have to forthrightly insist, and if necessary I will spell it out, E for English B for bloody E again but make if for effete or elderly this time, S for you know what I mean to say, that the name, as one of NATO's gentlemen to another, is C for . . .'

'Before you go any further', interposed his visitor, 'let me say that rarely, if ever, in the history of Anglo-American relations have I experienced so frank and yet friendly an etc. etc.'

'And give my best regards to Charles Dickens, should you see him', said Chewson as, not to be undone in amiability, he waved goodbye.

X

THE MUSE

A brawl is a brawl is a brawl

THE QUESTION has been asked, and it is repeated here because it was Lord Balfour who first asked it, whether it is possible to over-emphasize the role of the poet, the painter and the musician in the unfolding of English history and character. Have, in the past, historians devoted too scant attention to the solicitor, the brigadier, the bricklayer and the district nurse?

The late Earl Baldwin, himself a student of history, is reported to have remarked in his blunt fashion to the (later) Earl Attlee, then but winning his spurs in the rough yet essentially kindly tumble of English political life: 'Clem, you know you can't have common labour without common labourers'. To which, in a response already historic, the predestined leader of the Labour Party rejoined: 'But Stanley, never forget, as some of your friends on your side of the House are sometimes a little bit inclined to do, that the labourer is worthy of his hire'. 'Aha,' riposted the Conservative leader with his disarming chuckle, 'I see the devil can still quote scripture to his purpose,' and was thought to have had a shade the better of the verbal joust.

(Eagerly repeated in the Clubs and lobbies, the story, with its forthright disclosure of the Labour Crusader's essentially radical position, adopted after years of trial and error at Haileybury, lost him many a vote among the so-called 'moderates' of his party. But, as so often happens in England, Common Sense ultimately won through triumphant, and a temporary settlement was made, subject to rescission by the Board.)

Those who affect to see in the present day 'cult' of the moving picture actor (or the player of the 'ragtime' music so popular among the youth of our time) some new and possibly degenerate, or, at the best, debilitating influence, have (possibly through some lack of training in the true historical approach) surely failed to note that, whereas in the earlier Elizabethan Age two Earls and a rival dramatist not only shared the general idolization of Shakespeare but went to the length of 'planting' (if one may employ some useful Americanism) evidence to convince subsequent generations that they actually *were* Shakespeare and had written all but the more vapid and ill-constructed of his works, there are but few Peers at the present moment claiming actually to *be* Elvis Presley, Satchmo Armstrong, or Arthur Miller.

It is a measure of the progress that has been made by an England which, as has truly been said, 'started rather small, became somewhat bigger, and then got somewhat smaller again'. Sainte-Beuve in the 1850's found it necessary to remind the volatile French that 'it is hard to learn that one no longer has to govern the world'. In England a similar reminder would be otiose. It was almost certainly an Englishman who first said 'freedom is the recognition of necessity' and it is not untypical of the Slav outlook that Lenin – after an all-too cursory examination of the works available at the British Museum – should have issued this phrase as his own, causing needless embarrassment to a people which had known it all along but, for very obvious reasons, did not care to seem, even by implication, to be quoting Russians.

Progress there was, but it was slow, and – as has been seen in the fullness of the ultimate event – desirably so. Often enough in the history of the European community, as it must (except in case of destructive war between its component members) be termed, while the excitable Latin has cried '*Festina*', it is the deep steady bass of the Englishman which has appended the indispensable corrective '*lente*'.

In other words, English literature was not built in a day. Many were the obstacles which its fathers had to overcome. At the outset, for example, even the language was almost useless for the purpose, as Chaucer found to his cost. (It is much to the credit of the English that, though the greater part of what he wrote is unintelligible to the normal man or woman, he has been given the benefit of the doubt and been dubbed a 'poet'. One likes to think that after his many difficulties he would have been pleased to hear that this was so. 'Considering', he is reported to have said on his deathbed, 'that the language was in a state of flux, with all spellinges uncertaine, I did my best. I can think of no finer epitaff for an Englishman'.)

Brawling followed almost immediately and became a major hazard for English Poets. Christopher Marlowe was a case in point. Authorities have argued interminably as to whether he passed away in a tavern brawl, a brawl in a bawdy house, a brawl in a street, or in some undefined brawl occurring after breakfast. But no one doubted that the thing was a brawl. It is a measure of what the poets of that period had to face. . . . And whatever may be the final judgment of history on such poets as Shakespeare and Eliot, it is much to their credit that the former did not die in a brawl, and there is no evidence leading to anyone supposing that the latter will do so, either, despite the circumstance of having been, at one time, an associate of Ezra Pound, who, great poet though he be, had at a certain period a tendency towards the brawl. But he is, after all, an American, and thus outside the scope of our present study. English Poets soon saw that brawling was not the road forward. And, with the idea once grasped, they eschewed brawling. With the result that Stendhal, on his famous visit to England, noted that '*Le brawl*' had ceased to be a major feature of English Literary Life. (A situation fortunate, considering his physique, for Stendhal.)

At the outset of what may be termed – for want of a better phrase – English Literature, there already existed a profound and regrettable misunderstanding between the writing people and the State. Under the first Elizabeth, the Organization for General Popular Uplift (popularly abbreviated to OGPU), which was later transformed into the National Knowledge Verification Department (NKVD, as it came to be known in popular parlance), both took a mistaken attitude to writing men. For some extraordinary reason it was taken for granted by these authorities that men like Ben Jonson, the first poet-laureate, Bill Davenant and actually Dryden, needed, or at least wanted, drink more than almost anything else.

It was not until Alfred Lord Tennyson put a stop to the disgraceful practice by commuting the 'butt of sack' which had previously been paid to laureates into a cool cash payment of £27 (it is now known that it was in order to show the cheque – something of a windfall –

that he asked Maud into the garden, thus enriching Literature) that the notion of buying genius with alcoholic liquor finally ceased.

Nor were the tribulations of our British Poets, essayists, novelists, short-story writers and scripters yet at an end.

During the early nineteenth century the rent of garrets and attics rose steeply, and many a promising poet who, circa 1825, had settled down to starve in his garret or attic, found, before he could complete his snatch of genius, a wolf not merely at, but within, the door.

Browning took steps, and close on his heels W. Auden took some more. The latter's 'Wolves in attics, Recommended Treatment of' (Oxford University Press) is a little gem of its kind and provides more knowledge of English Literature than can be obtained from any similar book of like title.

It is a tribute to the English genius to be able to note that today no such difficulties confront the aspirant Englishman (or, one need hardly say, woman) who seeks to storm the heights of Abraham with an Elegy on the Playing Fields of Eton. In England the splendid men of the Cultural Inspiration Duty, and in the United States the Federation of the Brotherly Inspired, have seen to it that, as Earl Baldwin once said, 'the man who keeps reasonably close to the line now has a reasonably good chance of being close to the breadline when it comes'.

XI

SEX EXAMINED

Kinsey slept here

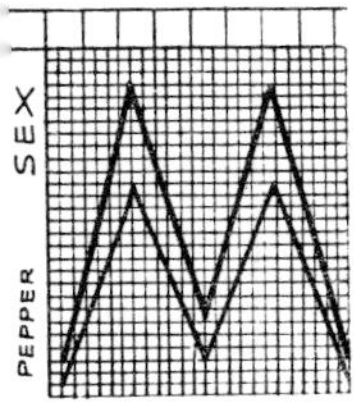

MODERN HISTORIANS – among them Vishniak of Tennessee and Œsterreich Ungarn of Los Angeles – attempting to evaluate patterns of long-term influence-pacts on English history, have rated sex second only to pepper which, as Trevelyan of Cambridge has shown, by being in short upply from the earliest times until the early nineteenth :entury, went far to necessitate the Empire. Later, as viser counsels prevailed and hot-heads were restrained, his institution became the Commonwealth of Nations.

There have been some, indeed, who – as a result of a nisunderstanding none the less deplorable for being in-.elligible – have sought to suggest that the English sex-ine, as such, was throughout more policy-determinative han the pepper-urge. (The findings of Stab, of Bonn, vho claimed that until 1803 there had been a confusion of the pepper-image with the papa-image, are brilliant out unsound. Freud specifically repudiated him.)

It is, however, true that a connection existed between .hese two influences or, as Twerp of Denver defines hem, 'the hither-thither-push-pulses'. Nautch girls, for :xample, were unknown to English thought and literature until discovered by agents of the East India Company who, as they proved in court, were genuinely out for pepper. On finding nautch girls they had, said counsel, stood aghast at their own moderation. Geisha girls followed for the same reason. A man who tried to make a joke in bad taste about a 'Spicy bit of goods' was expelled from the Far East and his licence endorsed.

'The scarcity,' notes Trevelyan, 'of fresh meat in winter before the era of roots and artificial grasses was a chief reason why our ancestors craved for spices,' particularly pepper. It was thus indeed fortunate that 'Turnip' Townsend did not succeed in popularizing winter fodder for cattle until it was too late to stop the conquest of India, and that the sturdy common sense of the English people rejected the specious propaganda of vegetarian doctrinaires, many of whom were of foreign origin. In an effort to create a diversion, the Dutch, knowing that if the English could get a chance to do some gardening they would drop everything else, introduced modern horticulture to the country in 1500. Wiser counsels prevailed. Had it been otherwise, England might be very nearly where it is now without ever having had Calcutta, etc., in the meantime.

Describing the price of pepper as 'frankly exorbitant', the Portuguese rounded the Cape of Good Hope to get more of it, and South Africa began, with its many consequences. (Vasco da Gama, however, proved in court that he had been genuinely right out of pepper.) The English Government immediately took steps to impose a sharply increased tax on the commodity. With ıe idea, apparently, of closing a gap, an influential roup of doctors declared that pepper caused Black)eath.

All this has suggested to superficial observers that the verage English man and woman of the period thought f nothing but pepper, to the exclusion of all other ıterests. Nothing could be farther from the truth.

In our day, when 'specialization' has been carried to vhat some thoughtful people consider dangerous ex-remes, it may be hard to evoke the picture of an age in vhich it was considered perfectly normal for a man who as interested in pepper to be interested in, for example, x as well. The units of personnel, as has been well ıid, of Tudor England were, in the fullest sense of the ord, 'all-rounders'. Not to be proficient in pepper-ading, sex, beating the bounds, mumming, sex, Nine Ien's Morris, bear-leading, secret diplomacy, cock-ghting, the ducking-stool, *petits-chevaux*, wassail, sex, ressage, rapine, witchcraft, sex, bowls and beard-ingeing was a mark of personal inadequacy, often ausing traumatic schizophrenia.

As regards sex, it is true that Henry VIII had brought he whole practice into widespread disrepute, and given ise to those efforts to have it suppressed altogether – ither, as some urged, by Act of Parliament, or, as others eemed sufficient, by the sheer weight of enlightened ublic opinion – which have continued with varying uccess right up to our own times. However, a Com-nission appointed to look into the matter ultimately eported that total prohibition would, in its opinion, in the long run have an adverse effect upon the continuing availability of personnel for, among other industries, the pepper trade, and the proposal was dropped.

Indeed, within a few years, sex was again so wide-spread that Elizabeth became an object of genera amazement simply by being a Virgin Queen. (In the same way the late Stanley Baldwin was distinguished from all preceding Prime Ministers by being known as 'honest'.)

Yet Queen Anne, who had seventeen children, wa known only as being the contemporary of a certain architectural style and – later – as being dead.

Many, Gladstone among them, believed that, with the trade routes to the Far East assured, steamships full of pepper available at every port, and the Married

Women's Property Act no longer a feminist dream but a solid fact, the traditional English character was doomed to suffer sharp deterioration. What, they asked, would become of young men who, now that they could get fresh meat all the year round, needed less pepper and had more of it than ever before, and were no longer inspired by the possibility of marrying some unsuspecting girl and immediately looting her of every penny she possessed? Might they not lose interest in women and the Empire alike, falling into a state of moral flaccidity only too reminiscent of the decadence of Rome?

Even the example of Parnell, with his vivid and abiding interest in, at least, the Irish part of the Empire and in Kitty O'Shea, failed wholly to reassure these prophets of disaster, particularly when, a good many years later, they overheard the late Lord Balfour murmur in his inimitable fashion that 'nothing matters much and very little matters at all'.

It was a shocking thing to say at the best of times, and it was not the best of times when he said it, for already the development of the aeroplane was imperilling England's insular security, and by 1913 the Trades Union Congress counted no less than 2⅛ million affiliated members. The writing was on the wall. It was, as the late Lord Northcliffe said, no time for complacency. Only a new moral purpose, and a rapid and steady development of the whisky industry against the day when it would be indispensable to the closing of the dollar gap, would suffice to carry the country through its hour of need.

Small wonder that there were many who looked back regretfully to the days before the introduction of competitive examination for the Civil Service had undermined the initiative of English youth, facing many young men with the alternative of open competition against others who might prove abler than themselves, or emigrating to Australia where they would be sneered at as 'Pommies' and be expected by their English relatives to make money, in some way, out of sheep.

In this time of growing disillusion, it was not to be expected that English sex would feel itself able to proceed in the old carefree way. In other words, it was a time of change. It was not too much to say that if Charles II had had an opportunity to peruse the works not only of the late H. G. Wells, but even of the early Arnold Bennett, he would have been vividly aware of an outlook on many problems and aspects of social life sharply differentiated from his own. Yet, within a few years, the German Emperor was to be toppled from his throne, and the late Ramsay MacDonald was to occur as the first Labour Prime Minister, albeit without a majority in the House of Commons.

XII

THE BASE

Bagehot speaks out

NO DEEP INSIGHT into English history is required for the realization that over a considerable period English men, women and – to a lesser extent – children showed a lively and (to our modern minds) sometimes almost hysterical interest in what hey seem to have thought of as The Constitution. Thus Bolger, in his *Diary of a Thoughtful Man's Journey in South Cumberland* (1901), notes that even at that late date he was able to interview a bicycle salesman whose father a formerly prosperous farmer ruined by the American Civil War and the Alabama Claims) could recall many a pithy tale of the Constitution and remark that in his day 'folk did use to bother their heads aboon it'.

Many critics have argued that the discussions, prolonged over many hundreds of years, as to whether this measure or that of English Government could or could not be deemed 'constitutional', were what would nowadays be termed a 'waste of time'.

The answer is that they would seem a waste of time to us now, today, but did not seem so to them, then. It may even be asked whether, in their simple beliefs and assumptions on the subject, they were not – in their

admittedly naïve way, happier than those who, in ou
own day, have been brought up to see the Constitutio
simply and clearly as a charming and thoroughly worth
while piece of pageantry, having a particular appeal t
visitors from overseas.

(It may be noted in passing that whereas on the ev
of the Boer War the main influx of Constitution
conscious students came to England's shores fron
France and Germany – many of them, regrettably, dis
sidents, seeking in the British Constitution grounds fo
criticism of their own – today the overwhelmin
majority is from Universities west of the Mississippi an
east of the Niger, bringing the keen eye of the pioneer, th
sharp view of the uninhibited, and the all-too welcom
guerdon of the dollar. As a thoroughly modern-minde
Chancellor of the Exchequer – as he then was – M
Macmillan, in one of those sallies which later made hin
famous, and feared, as a rapier wit, is reported to hav
said: 'Say what you like, the Constitution pays off'.)

There was of course a time – most of it before th
Scots began to give their full attention to the possibilitie
of English history – when Englishmen paid less attentio
to the Constitution than they did to the Second Law c
Thermodynamics. And if the matter was brought t
their attention, as it was after the unfortunate reign o
King John, they realized – as every political man
woman and civil servant realizes today – that whateve
the Constitution might be, it could without mucl
difficult be changed or circumvented by brute force
expert assassination, skilful chicanery, crude chicanery

nixed chicanery, or what the late Lloyd George used to lescribe, according to a reported remark of the late ord Oxford, as 'the glorious lassitude of desuetude'.

In this connection there is an interesting and sig-ificant account in Bluntschli's *History of the Relations etween Monarchy, People and Constitution in Latter Day England* (published by the Kaiser Wilhelm's Institut in uly, 1914) of how the late Lord Balfour, at the height f the Home Rule Bill crisis, attempted to report this emark to the late Edward VII.

Lapsing into the vernacular, the monarch replied: *Pfui Teufel*, these *verdammter* Welsh', and Lord Balfour – who was well able to combine tact with hilosophy, and was in any case deeply concerned with he impending railway strike which some thought rossly unconstitutional – withdrew in order, later, to epeat the tale to George V, who remarked: 'What the Devil's the matter with that damned Welshman?'

Thus the precious English quality of continuity was ssured. And when Edward VIII, on a famous occasion, ommented apropos of Lord Baldwin: 'What in hell oes that man who makes his money out of Welsh steel, ut lives on the English side of the Border, think he's laying at?' he was, as has been too little realized, only eeking to carry on the old tradition.

Those who assume that the long-drawn interest in the Constitution, culminating in the unlucky dispute be-ween Charles I and others, and taking a further turn in s typically quiet, but assured, English course when the nglish, in 1688, realizing that their traditions, the very heart of their Anglicism, were at stake, assisted a Dutchman to chase a Scotsman down the river, thus giving themselves time to look about and find a German to take over their monarchy, did not do much ultimate good, are almost certainly mistaken.

It gave employment to many, and caused many others, who were merely engaged in plundering a monastery or manor house, in committing rapine on the

Making Enquiry of a Partie of Gentlemen whether they are For or Against or Don't Know about the Constitution

lower orders or other activities, to understand that they were doing so in favour of, or against, a change in the Constitution.

And it cannot be too often emphasized that, without these ideological stimulants to action, very little is likely to be done.

It was left to the Victorians – cynical, dissolute, and

blivious of the vast forces of history which were building up under and around them – to knock the final hips out of the foundations of the Constitution.

There had been, a hundred and more years earlier, 'oltaire. There had been the French Encyclopædists in eneral. They were, as is known, cynical, dissolute, and as Maidstrom has rightly said – 'force-oblivious'. The esult was the French Revolution and much that that nplies.

The Victorians refused to be forewarned. Led by hoteads like Walter Bagehot, who in 1867 published his 'ork on the *English Constitution*, they set out – conciously or unconsciously – to undermine the faith itherto firmly rooted in the hearts of men.

Which of these first and finally implanted the idea iat the English Constitution was *unwritten* – in other 'ords, that everyone in power could make it up as he ent along – is fortunately not known. For a while the nglish, not realizing the appalling blow that had been ealt to their faith, accepted this notion with equanimity even boasting of it to foreigners, who came over to ngland trying to compare the paragraphs of their onstitutions with that of the English and found the isk impossible.

'Not written' was the English response to these lvances, and very little exchange of opinion could, as a esult, be made. And for several years the idea that, hereas everyone in France and the United States knew hat they had by way of a Constitution, no one in ngland had any possibility of knowing any such thing,

seemed to English people a subject for actual self
applause.

With the later development of the Civil Service, wit
the rise of Left-Realism – at one time threatening, unti
it was balanced by Right-Realism – it became apparen
to pensive observers that the Constitution is bette
served by being presented in the annual pageantry c
the Lord Mayor's Show (which had its origin in th
days when kings durst scarce show their faces in th
crowd of jostling apprentices 'twixt Westminster and th
City, as Ogilvie has so trenchantly pointed out) than i
any other way.

'Otherwise,' as a future Lord Chancellor has said, 'i
may be necessary to change it, in which case it woul
hardly be the Constitution as we have all grown t
know it.'

That, it may be said, is a typical upsummation of a
attitude to a question, and, as such, well worth study b
all students of English history.

XIII

HAPPY FAMILIES

'Wid' me bundle on me shoulder'

THE FAMILY is nearly inseparable from sex, and, according to the late Andrew Lang, 'the nicknames "Naked Dogs", "Liars", "Buffalo Dung", "Men who do not Laugh", "Big Topknots", have been thoroughly accepted by the "gentes" of the Blackfoot Indians'. That is so much to the good, and when we realize that in writing of 'gentes' in his anthropological manner Lang has reference to what is nowadays termed 'the family', we find ourselves almost at once in the midst of the basic English conception of The Family or Home which, as has been attested by many investigators, has played, and one might venture to say still does play, a part in what might be loosely defined as English 'family' or 'home' life.

On page 41 of his book *The Loyal and the Disloyal*, Morton Grodzins remarks of the family that its 'members frequently come face to face, and strongly identify themselves as a unit, whose rules of behavior are relatively informal and whose solidarity remains high despite the existence of strong internal dissension'. Strange though it may seem to some that an American, whose works are published by the University of Chicago

Press, should have obtained such insight into English folkways, it remains a verifiable fact that with the contraction of the Overseas Empire, formerly gone to by young members of families; the increase in currency restrictions now reducing to drabness the colourful existence of the old-time remittance man whose quaintly plaintive cry for 'a little more' once competed in every foreign street with the nostalgic strains of 'Alexander's Ragtime Band'; an over-all money shortage leading to non-ability to pay boarding, as distinct from day, school fees; the practice of holding Trade Union meetings on the job rather than of an evening; the intimidating length of the queue at the Divorce Courts; and the housing shortage which, though indispensable to the politician, can on occasion be irksome to the individual, members of English families do, in fact, 'frequently come face to face'.

There are sociologists who see in this development the seeds of decay. Yet it probably would be truer to say that what we have here is one more example of the essential continuity of English life. Those who have, from time to time, assumed the housing shortage, for example, to be a comparatively modern phenomenon, simply have not lived in the Middle Ages. At that period it was indeed true that the Englishman's home was his castle, in the sense that, unless moated, battlemented, and properly fitted with slits for the outpouring of boiling oil, the family residence was not so much a home as a mere dwelling place, subject to any moment to arson, rapin, and *jus primae noctis*. It was thus left almost xclusively to the well-to-do to lay the foundations of the home', a circumstance which was to affect the haracter of English family life for many generations to ome. But it is also true that as a result of these circumtances the castle, particularly in areas where there was axity – as there all too often was – on the part of the Iealth authorities, was frequently grossly over-crowded. Vhole families stayed in it merely because there was no ther safe place to go. And even so they could not be ertain of having the constricted space available to hemselves. For it was at any time open to a dependent ovel-dweller to report hostile arsonists and rapists on he move and seek safety within the castle walls.

Admittedly, in consequence of the undue and, as it nust seem to the modern man, almost neurotic imortance attached to salt, it was possible to preserve ome sort of order by arranging for certain types of inlividual to sit below it. What was not noticed by, often nough, even 'liege' Lords was that the air-intake of hose below the salt was *to all intents and purposes* equivaent to that of those above it. In those days, as now, rchitects were behind the times and it was many a long ear before they had the wit to move from the early to he later Norman style, or even to grasp that just beause the French of that period were unable to disinguish between a *cheminée*, meaning fireplace, and a himney, in the proper sense of the word, there was no eason for Englishmen to follow their example. They herefore built no chimneys, stating that the smoke vould, as so many accounts of the period phrase it, 'find its way up' to a hole in the roof. It was the type o assumption which brought English architects into ba repute. Later, they were to make things worse, so far a

their reputation was concerned, by building London i such a way that it burned to the ground in what wa described by a contemporary as 'a veritable holocaust' by putting waterpipes outside instead of inside build- ings, so that they froze and burst; and by making a lon series of mistakes about what to do with the oppor- tunities offered by the activity of the German Air Force

Smoke-choked and jostled as, probably, never before many an Englishman allowed his thoughts to turn t ways and means of getting away from home. It must however, be remembered, that women were not wha they are, so that it was not until the invention of th chastity belt that those dreams which had caused so many an English spring-tide could be translated into the reality of the Crusades. It was then that, for the first time, 'Mr Englishman' felt justified in taking that trip to the Middle East he had so often contemplated. It made, as the saying went, 'a nice change'.

In this connection it ought to be realized that the controversial character of the motivations responsible for the crusades was not fully understood by those who took part in them. Asked whether economic pressures or religious fanaticism seemed to be uppermost in his mind as he adjusted his red cross and swung into the saddle, the average crusader was all too apt to take refuge in some equivocal statement about 'getting a breath of fresh air' or 'broadening the mind', or else simply to mumble in the manner which originally gave rise to the legend of the strong silent Englishman. The fact seems to have been that a good many men of that period did not know, or even much care, what, in the modern psychiatric phrase, 'made them tick'. They were apt to say '*sum*' without appreciating the need for the preliminary '*cogito, ergo*'. They were, in the most literal sense of the phrase, living in the Middle Ages.

The full effect of the crusades upon the English character will always be a matter for speculation and argument. M. Charles Seignobos in his *Rise of European Civilization* states, about as tentatively as a statement can be stated, that 'the apricot, water-melon and shallot seem to have come from the Holy Land'. More assuredly he gives it as his definite view that the crusades caused beards. Whether they also were responsible for 'the decline of piety through contact with the Moslems of Syria' he very rightly regards as 'questionable'.

Henri Pirenne, in his *History of Europe*, reports that in order to 'excite' people to go crusading, Pope Urban had found it necessary to employ propagandists who 'vaunted, in one breath, the quantity of relics to be found in Asia Minor, the charm and luxury of its customs, and the beauty of its women'. To this early conditioning is probably attributable the attraction which, until very recent times, the Middle East has had for the English tourist, and also the disillusionment which has affected those who, half-way through the tour, came to the conclusion that the women of that region were just 'not their type'.

Moreover, although Bohemund of Tarento, and those nice Bouillon brothers, Godfrey and Baldwin, made charming and sophisticated travelling companions, the question may be asked whether their influence on the English was altogether good. The continentals, with the best will in the world, did not always realize what the lure of Antioch could do to a knight who previously had never been outside a moat-girt demesne in Norfolk.

However, despite these distracting influences, the family held together, often busying itself making a crypt and effigy against the potential non-return of the warrior. And family manners soon became more civilized. People still went on referring to their neighbours as 'naked dogs', 'liars' and 'buffalo dung', but did so only in private.

As, with the passage of centuries, times became

quieter, the English were more and more insistently confronted with the problem of younger sons, who, in earlier and perhaps harsher times had been wont to fall in battle. Other nations saw no difficulty in dividing up the family property equally between all the sons. The English grasped at once that this would be a mistake. It would, to mention but one disadvantage, hamper the development of the Empire. The obvious thing to do was to give the eldest son everything, the rest nothing but a warm-hearted blessing and a copy of any good collection of fairy stories (that same Andrew Lang made several) showing that, although he starts out with nothing, it is usually the third of the three brothers who makes good in the end.

Much attracted by this type of reading matter, the lads went off to the Indies with little if any demur.

It is significant of the power and warmth of English home-sense that, throughout a great part of the nineteenth century, British officials in India, first under the East India Company – known as 'John' Company in recognition of its simple, forthright honesty – and later under the Empire, were given one year's leave in each four years, *on condition* that they did not spend it anywhere west of Suez. It was feared that on sighting the gabled roofs of The Towers, Tonbridge, they might decide to sit down in the garden with Mom, leaving India to govern, develop or loot itself.

It must be admitted that during the early part of this period – probably under the debilitating influence of the eighteenth century when a good many non-specifically-English practices had crept in – there was a tendency for boys to use the home as their dwelling and life-centre until quite late in their 'teens. In other words, the home was cheapened by being taken for granted. So far as the well-to-do were concerned, this tendency was corrected by the invention of the public school. And for those adult males who could not, for some reason or other, go to India, the development of the Club offered the same opportunity to maintain a proper reverence for the home by staying away from it.

In fairness to the working classes, it should be pointed out that for many years the fact that these amenities were beyond their reach caused many of them to treat an almost communal type of family life as a matter of course. Even the public house was often visited by the whole family together. Even in our own day, except during the War years when the Government had powers to 'direct' labour in a sensible way to wherever it was needed, this attitude persisted, with the result that when men became redundant in one place they often hesitated to move at once to some place where work was available even a couple of hundred miles away on the ground that they 'did not want to leave their families and could not find accommodation for them' anywhere near the new work-site.

Although there were pessimists who felt that only a very large and, as it seemed, momentarily impracticable expansion of overseas forces would correct this ideology, the general belief was that education would gradually find a way.

XIV

LEADERSHIP

Its risks and opportunities

IT IS A COMMONPLACE, noted by many historians in tracing England's rise to her present pre-eminence, that not once nor twice in the island's history, there seemed to loom the possibility that some other nation might forge disastrously ahead in the race for the moral leadership of the world.

Spain, after the final collapse or disintegration of her overseas Empire was excellently placed, particularly as there seemed little prospect of her maintaining for long the value of her currency, and those of her politicians who were not corrupt displayed a uniform mediocrity in face of the problems confronting the country. It is true that a number of Commanders, shatteringly defeated in the field, on the high seas, and in diplomacy, returned from Uruguay and Cuba declaring that the boundaries of Spain's cultural influence had thereby been extended, and her spiritual authority immeasurably enhanced, but they were ahead of their time. Public opinion in the Iberian Peninsula was not ready to receive their message. Spain, in other words, had not had the advantage of what may be called 'the English experience of trial and error'. Indeed, in an attempt to adopt English ideas without properly assimilating them, Spaniards often dealt with things in the wrong order, conceiving that error should be followed by trial, with the death penalty frequently ensuing soon after.

As the late Ernest Bevin and Lord Rothermere are said to have remarked to Professor Madariaga and the Duke of Alba: 'The tragedy of Spain, viewed *sub specie aeternitatis* – if we do not stand open to a charge of solecism by thus relating the mundane to the essentially imponderable – is that you fellows never had Labour and Tory and all that'.

With typical *caballerismo*, Professor and Duke acknowledged the inward justice of the criticism.

More dangerous than what has been termed 'the Spanish challenge' was, from the English standpoint, the threat to moral and cultural world leadership offered by the United States during the first years of the first Wilson Administration.

Never – so it seemed to thinking men and women of the time – had any country (not even England under Charles II) found itself in a happier position, or one more likely to ensure that its views would carry decisive weight in the councils of a distracted world.

The gold reserves were low, and getting lower by the month. There was but moderate confidence in the stability of the dollar which, shaky for years, fell – under the stresses of 1914 – to the inspiring level of six dollars seventy-eight cents to the pound sterling on the first day of August that year.

For the greater part of the two years immediately

following Wilson's election, the country owed more money than anyone thought it could possibly pay. Encouraging in itself, this state of affairs was rendered even happier by the knowledge that the President was an obdurate doctrinaire, and the Secretary of State, William Jennings Bryan, a man who was swept to power on a tide of gross misunderstanding about the nature of money, and held equally grotesque views on almost

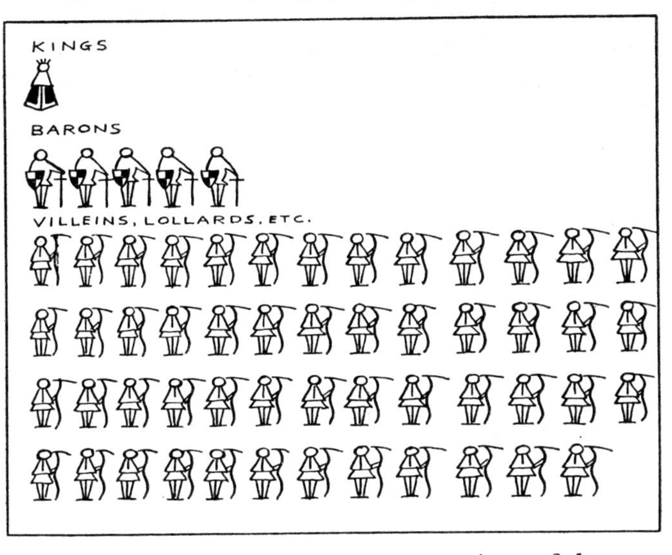

every other subject within the purview of human thought.

He was well served by a Diplomatic Corps no one of whose members noticed that war was about to break out in Europe until a few hours before it happened.

Suffice it simply to add that the Army and Navy, so

often an obstacle to moral leadership, were at a particularly low ebb. A few battleships had been built, but the fleet as a whole was no match for anyone. The entire Army had four modern field guns, but luckily means for transporting them from one place to another had not been provided by the contractors.

On the labour front strikes were continuous and widespread.

The American failure to grasp the possibilities thus offered have been attributed by embittered American critics alike to the impetuosity of President Wilson and his advisers who – on noting that the German and Irish vote in South Chicago and North Pittsburgh seemed to be no longer decisive, concluded that the moment had come to save democracy and the British Empire from the Kaiser – and to the reputed cunning of British policy.

However that may have been, forty years and one and a half World Wars later, moral and cultural leadership had passed to England.

Regarded in the perspective of history this can be seen as no 'flash in the pan'. England's progress, often slow, occasionally devious, had nevertheless been steady. Lord North Day, with its traditional ceremonies, annually brings home to English schoolchildren the significance of the achievement of that almost visionary statesman who saw that what carping critics of the period – including the notorious Boston Group – referred to as the 'loss' of the American colonies, was a priceless boon, and, indeed, a *sine qua non* of development towards the brotherhood of the English-speaking peoples.

And it should be remembered that even Dr Jameson, whose 'raid' did so much, in its small way, to prepare the future path of South African evolvement towards its present constructive relationship towards, within, and – when occasion demands – without the Commonwealth, was the object of much vulgar and ill-informed criticism.

The examples of Australia, New Zealand and – to a lesser extent – Canada are sometimes cited by hostile analysts of the English political genius as examples of a failure to get rid of acquisitions, with all that such failure implies in terms of moral authority. In the case of Australia, it must be admitted by the honest historian that mistakes were made.

That having been said, it must also be admitted that the mistakes were natural. They resulted from the effort to carry out a plan, excellent in itself, without sufficient resources. The idea of, first, employing all the savagery of brutal laws to reduce a section of the English population to enforced criminality and then sending the 'criminals' concerned to start populating a continent, was in itself a boldly imaginative one. And one cannot, by hindsight, blame those responsible for the belief that England was not going to hear from the Australians again – except possibly as allies of the Japanese. We know now, of course, what went wrong. The number of criminals was inadequate. But the responsibility for this state of affairs must surely be laid not on the shoulders of the English people, but rather at the door of the under-organized police and judicial system.

Those who seek, nowadays, to impugn English moral status at the United Nations on the ground that England occasionally enjoys the 'unfair' support of people from the Antipodes should realize that even the most eager advocates of devolutionary evolution cannot entirely, and at once, disentangle themselves from the unfortunate legacies of history.

The case of Canada is quite otherwise, and no survey of English history can afford to neglect it and its lessons.

The dislikes and, indeed, mutual loathing of the English-speaking Canadians for the French-speaking ones, combined with their common contempt for the Americans and the mother-country – a contempt shared by that section of English opinion which for many years supposed Canada to be populated exclusively by remittance-men and absconding debtors – sufficed for a long period to maintain the population of that Dominion at a conveniently low level.

Later, with the introduction of the Geiger counter – said to have been smuggled into Alberta by a disaffected Indian trader in search of 'fire-water' – there began to be more Canadians than hitherto.

To the faint-hearted, this was alarming. But it was soon realized that their fears were groundless. There were times when the Canadians supported English policies, proving that blood was thicker than water. There were others when Canada boldly opposed, or at least abstained from supporting, the English line, and showed a fine, imaginative readiness to sell to the United States whatever resources might be available.

These episodes were particularly welcome at Westminster, as proof of the essential flexibility of the English genius.

And the same thing, as Clive was far-sighted enough to note, applies to India.

XV

UPSHOT

'History's Tote Double' exclaims Observer

IN A MOVE which already has done much to streamline history, Reiman, of Chicago, has pointed out that societies – certainly western societies – have been successively 'tradition-directed', 'inner-directed', and 'other-directed'. His gadget is now in regular use by thousands of satisfied thinkers, some of whom claim it has cut their thinking-time *by as much as 22 per cent*. And many people are asking themselves: Why did no one produce this valuable yet essentially simple idea before? Many have been reminded of Emerson and the mouse-trap which, if a man made a better one, would cause millions to make a path to his door, or words to that effect. Until someone offers a better explanation, it seems probable that we shall have to make do with this one.

Reiman's device can be of the highest utility in finally summing up the course of English history. Indeed it has been said that until it became generally available to delvers and summarizers, they were doomed to slow and shoddy production, with declining exports. Foreign students, wanting, for instance, a quick, serviceable evaluation of the rise of the Tudors, often complained that delivery dates were not only late, but could not be guaranteed at all. Naturally they went elsewhere for their information – sometimes even beyond the Iron Curtain. A sturdily constructed Marxist analysis of the relationship between the decline of the wool trade and early English tendencies to Protestantism, for example, put together in Prague has enjoyed a steady and expanding market in Africa and many other areas where formerly one rarely saw anything on the thought-ways but Trevelyans, Rowses and other well known English makes.

Enterprising English thinkers believe that all that can now be changed – provided the necessary initiative and imagination are not lacking.

Using the R-method, we can at once see that during the period when the English were tradition-directed, their thoughts and behaviour – what, in two words, have been described as their 'life-attitudes' – were directed by tradition. Religious beliefs played a major role. And these beliefs were of a Roman Catholic character – so much so that people did not both to refer to them as 'Roman' Catholic, but simply as 'Catholic'. (A good way of finding out when 'tradition direction' gave place to 'inner direction' is to ascertain when the phrase 'Roman Catholic' first started to come into general use. The date is not accurately known.)

The assassination of prominent prelates, which was not infrequent, the scurrilous and often obscene satirisation of the clergy in general, and the widespread practice of witchcraft, devil-worship and Manicheeism, not to mention an attitude of total scepticism frequently found in what we have termed the 'higher baron brackets', should not be allowed to affect the argument.

'Either', an R-method-demonstrator pointed out recently, 'these were already *part* of the religious tradition referred to, in which case there is nothing to worry about, and the frictional noises heard are normal to the functioning of the mechanism, or else these were exceptions which, by indicating the violence of the reaction against tradition, conclusively prove the strength of the tradition itself. Again, nothing to worry about. In either case, we have the Middle Ages good and taped and can get on to where society became inner-directed.'

From the viewpoint of the average thought-user, 'inner-directedness' is often found to be the most attractive of the three forms of directedness on offer.

After all, accepting a tradition seems, as the late Max Beerbohm is reported to have said in the course of an argument about science fiction with the late H. G. Wells, 'sort of sloppy'. Several bishops of the time were 'sloppy' thinkers, not willing to think things out for themselves and see what was wrong with their system as well as what, to quote Bernard of Quorum, looked like 'a bit of all right'. And later, as Wells was not slow to point out, there was 'bloody' Mary.

By her day, of course, inner-directedness had begun. Inner-directed people, according to those who prefer them, were wont to think for themselves and be motivated by strong moral considerations. They used to make it a rule to work out the difference between right

nd wrong and then do what was right. Latimer was
ke that, and when being burned at the stake in 1554
as not too nonplussed to coin a really excellent phrase
bout lighting a candle which would never be put out.
lis statement was much appreciated by his companion
adversity, Ridley, who, while he could say things him-
elf – he had said, for instance, some time before, that in
is opinion the girl who was later (though he was not
a position to know that) to become Queen Elizabeth,
as quite definitely illegitimate – was generous enough
recognize good things even when said by others.

'Inner-directed' people thus had active enquiring
ninds, and were responsible for science. Those who
went in for' science during the tradition-directed
eriod at first seemed to present an anomaly. Once
gain, however, it can be seen that they were either
xceptions proving rules, or else mere pseudo-scientists,
erging on alchemy.

Nevertheless, it has to be admitted that association
vith scientists has to some extent damaged the other-
vise high reputation of inner-directed people and
eriods. From very early times, starting indeed right
utside England, there has been a good deal of suspicion
f scientists for some of which they must themselves be
eld responsible.

It has not been forgotten here – some of our friends in
he United States seem to have rather shorter memories,
hough of course there has been a lot of exaggeration –
hat when the people of Athens were going through a
ery difficult period, standing alone against hordes and

trying to do democracy at the same time, scientist Democritus saw fit to state that 'according to convention there is a sweet and a bitter, and a hot and a cold and according to convention there is colour. In truth there are atoms and a void.'

It was pretty generally felt that, as our French friends who really have been simply splendid throughout would say, he had 'missed an excellent opportunity to keep his mouth shut'.

It had been forcefully argued that Democritus was not a 'typical' scientist, and it is known that many Greek scientists with a lot more on the ball than D. but without his itch for publicity, deliberately refrained from making this kind of statement at the time because they knew it to be unhelpful. As a result of this attitude on the part of decent physicists and such, people who had been scared by Democritus gradually came to lose their fear of scientists, and to realize that for every one of them shouting about voids there were five working on a constructive plan for sewage disposal at the Piræus.

There are, indeed, those who claim that scientists would have been in optimum odour from then on had it not been for Sir Francis Bacon. And there is a modicum of justice in the claim.

One is not of course referring to his private life, nor even to the part – to say the least of it equivocal – which he played in the Who Wrote Shakespeare row, but rather to the fact that to the general (and admittedly uninstructed) public he gave the impression of being a flibbertigibbet – as, for instance, in his absurdly misleading views on the laws of aerial flight. Here was a man ostensibly talking about aeroplanes, but when you look at what he said – stuff about the 'weight in the nose' and so on – you can see that all you could construct from his specifications would be a paper dart.

The same frivolous-looking, 'just-ladle-in-the-hydrogen-and-see-what-happens' attitude, a reputation for which has done scientists so much harm, was apparent in Bacon's shot at inventing deep freeze. There he was in a snowdrift at the bottom of Highgate Hill, and he got this idea that if you stuffed a hen with snow it might be preserved as well as if preserved in salt. He had the element of a truth there, of course. But instead of thinking it over quietly, he jumps out of the cab, buys a hen from a woman who has a chicken-run there, messes about in the snow, stuffing it, and drives home with the thing dripping on to his lap. Naturally he caught a chill and it killed him. That was not the scientific spirit; that was irresponsibility.

And, what's more, it was infectious, and you got a man like Edmund Wyld, who lived in Bloomsbury and probably did more to bring both science and that quarter of London into disrepute with the British public than any man before or since. Anyone who has ever appealed for funds to establish a new foundation for British nuclear research knows that there is always somebody in the audience who says: 'Surely we don't want to have a lot of Edmund Wylds fooling with the fission' – and that is how other nations take the lead.

As is the case with so many scientists, nutrition was one of the things Wyld was on about, and he used to bet people that, given six months, he could prepare a bed of soil which would produce wheat without any seed being sown in it. Nobody actually took him on, but the extravagance of the claim did nothing to affirm people's faith in scientists as a responsible body of men.

According to John Aubrey, who was a friend of Wyld and sponged on him for years, after the Great Fire of London 'somebody' (an unknown scientist, it was supposed) poked a hole in the coffin of, of all people, John Colet, famous, long defunct Dean of St Paul's. Hearing of this episode, Wyld, and a maker of scientific instruments named Randolph Greatorex, first started to dabble in the embalming fluid and then, in what was at once seen as a typical 'spirit of scientific ıquiry', probed with a 'stick which they thrust into a hinke'. They reported that the body 'felt like boyld rawne'.

Apart from occasionally opening the door to scientific xcess, inner-directedness, which might otherwise have ome to stay indefinitely, suffered severely from the fact hat although those who took it up worked hard, and ften accurately, to get at the difference between right nd wrong, they came – too often for comfort or erenity – to different, and even opposite, conclusions. ometimes they seemed to contradict not only others, ut themselves.

Oliver Cromwell, a very fair specimen of inner-irectedness, was a case in point. He was kind to Jews provided they did not cause riots by over-publicising heir views), said that he would rather the whole ountry turned Moslem than that liberty of conscience hould be unduly interfered with, besought some of his ssociates, in a somewhat highly coloured phrase, 'in the owels of Christ' to consider whether they might not be nistaken, and attempted to exterminate the Irish Catholics by the most brutal massacres seen anywhere efore the twentieth century. He was thus a major in-luence on Anglo-Irish relations, which, fortunately it nay seem to some, are beyond the scope of this study. But there is small doubt that, if inner-directedness is to-lay less esteemed in Ireland than elsewhere, Cromwell ears a large share of the blame.

Inner-directedness was particularly rife in Scotland – circumstance which might have been irrelevant to

English history as such, had the Scots been content t
keep their attitude to themselves. In the event, the
could not resist seeking to export their theories c
religion and politics, with effects upon, for example, th
English monarchy and the Civil War which caused dis
may among those who had pinned their hopes to th
possibilities of peaceful co-existence.

The seeds of decay of the inner-directional syster
which once had seemed so promising, were thus alread
sprouting visibly. And, as so often happens in history
since the people concerned did not *at the time* know tha
what they were was inner-directed, they were not in
position effectively to combat the trend towards other
directedness.

Inner-directedness, it is true, lingered on in variou
forms through the eighteenth century and right into th
nineteenth. Indeed one of the difficult problems tha
has to be faced is to ascertain when it stopped and other
directedness set in. All that can be said with assurance i
that by not long ago it was here; in a form, too, clea
enough to be susceptible of analysis in Chicago.

The first point to get clear is that not everyone i
England is 'other-directed' in the bad sense of the term
(and, regrettable though the fact may be, most of its sense
are bad, and some of them worse). People who can spo
other people being subject to other-direction have, *e
hypothesi* – almost, one might venture to say, *ipso facto*
some of the better qualities of the tradition-directed, an
all the good, as distinct from dubious, ones of the inner
directed. They think for themselves, clearly and fearlessly

They know the difference between right and wrong. And for this very reason they cannot but note that the majority of their fellow citizens are in a sad way.

As the late Lord Balfour said of the spread of the (then) halfpenny press, mass production, socialism and the like, 'I don't at all like, the way things are going'.

What a number of American Professors, all excellent but too numerous for individual mention, have described as The Group is the big thing in other-directedness. It seems that (with the exception of the thinkers referred to above) most people have stopped thinking for themselves about anything, but instead of getting, at least, a tradition of some kind to keep them on the rails, they simply accept The Group – Group standards, Group thinking etc. etc. – as their criterion.

The result, one need hardly say, has been totalitarianism, Keeping up with the Joneses, mass-hysteria, passive assumption of the truth of statements an individual has not adequately tested, television, drab uniformity, the Welfare State, and espionage.

Grodzins, in the book already quoted, indeed sees other-directedness as a major factor in spy-business, because you get a man, otherwise loyal, who becomes a member of a – to take a single example – Society for the Promotion of the Philippine Sugar Industry, and soon all he cares about in life is winning and then retaining the good opinion of the Vice-Presidents of that Society. Before long, he is in and out of the Tate and Lyle factories in London and elsewhere, trying to steal valuable secrets for the men in Manila.

Naturally enough, the knowledge that other direction is now on, has a depressing effect upon the younger generation. They realize that they are up against something entirely new in English history. Devout villeins may have had their problems, but, if and when starvation or the Black Death came along, they knew full well that the tradition was, as the late President Woodrow Wilson and the early Editor of *The Times* have said, 'still in there, doing its old stuff'. Maimed by the explosion of uncontrolled gases, poisoned by experimental medicaments mixed by wild-eyed apothecaries in a hurry to join the teenage mob screaming for a touch of Burbage's doublet after the Globe first-night of *The Tempest*, men and women of, for instance, the first Elizabethan Age had their problems too, but they knew full well that their mental curiosity was going like a buzz-saw.

In those periods uniformity, except in dress, speech, general outlook and the hope of getting rather more money next year, was non-existent. Treachery and espionage had not been thought of. Sex, which in the latest period, caused extreme complications, was not merely not irksome, as now, but caused madrigals, noble and poetically phrased dramatic works, and, when necessary, inspiring self-sacrifice.

Probably more particularly embittering to the youth of England today is the realization that the people of these earlier periods did not appreciate their good luck. 'They had it good,' as Earl Baldwin said, 'and the b . . . s didn't know it'.

Yet, as anyone who has followed the steady pulse-eats of English history through the years must feel, the arkest cloud before dawn has a silver lining. 'Et hoc', 'ergil, himself a premature Englishman, observed, neminisse juvabit'. His very deep and sincere feeling, ne which coloured his whole attitude to life and to me extent accounted for his unpopularity with a lot of eople who felt, on a given day, less joyous than he, and ented their jealous bile by writing 'Vergil is a syco-hantic snob' on the walls of the all-too public lavatories hich were all that Rome (known to some as 'the lfare State') could offer the common citizenry, was, as xpressed in these words, that though it may seem a ttle hard to take now, we shall have a good laugh about later.

The value of looking back, it has been truly said, is to ach one to look forward. If the average number of vilized people annually tortured and violently done to eath in the twentieth century sharply exceeds that ttained in early periods; if it be true that an atomic fall-ut over, say, Birmingham could cause rather more ouble in a week than the old, haphazard, bubonic lague used to achieve in a couple of years, this may ell be the proof that quite soon things are going to ove in a different and, in some ways, more alluring irection. English history, as we have seen, is full of ich directional shifts. Just as one set of people was oming to the conclusion that it was due to be oppressed, assacred and preached at for ever, the shift came, and was able to grasp the hardly-dreamed-of opportunity

to oppress, massacre and preach on its own accoun
As the old Somersetshire proverb has it: 'Long thoug
a given lane may be, a turning will occur, unless ci
cumstances are exceptional'.

It is an inspiring thought, and Englishmen toda
would do well to paste in their hats for safe keeping.

XVI

PEASANTRY & POLIZEI

A mistake Marx 'hushed up'

IN A TOP-LEVEL SUMMATION of argument around what we may approximately term 'Darwin', Professor Julian Huxley has recently gone on record with the statement that, so far from there being any big mistake about non-purposeful evolution, 'the real wonder of life is the fact that e automatic and non-purposeful biological evolution ould eventually have generated true purpose, in the rson of the human species'.

Mutatis mutandis, and making full allowance for the ct that Professor Huxley was writing about something se, his statement may usefully be wrenched from its ntext and borne in mind by the student of English story. For it may well be considered that the real onder of that is that its confused, and often deplorable, ocesses should eventually have generated a true storic situation in the shape of the present day.

However distasteful may be some aspects of the past – one would attempt to palliate more than some arply restricted sectors of, for example, the thirteenth ntury – the essential is to remember that if actions and stitutions in the past had not been what they were, isting institutions might well be other than they are.

The history of the police force is a profoundly significant case in point. If, for example, we examine th
police force of the fourteenth century, we find that th
principal point to note about it is that it did not exis
And the same is true of the fifteenth to mid-nineteent
centuries, inclusive.

That the only 'police' organization in mid-eighteent
century London should have been placed under th
direction of a middle-aged novelist crippled by gout
a measure of the frivolity with which the problem wa
approached. It is worth noting that no English noveli
since Fielding has held or even – so far as is known
been offered the command of the Metropolitan Polic
And novelists of our own day, many of them with circu
lations far greater than Fielding's, accept the situatio
without demur. Thus progress goes on its way.

Professor Trevelyan pertinently suggests that, had th
English character been less good than it was, lootin
riots and mayhem would have been even more commo
than they were. This seems to be almost certainly th
truth. Yet, as the police and prison expert Major A. G
Griffiths remarks, crime at the end of the eighteent
century was 'rampant'. Burglaries were 'of consta
occurrence'. (In this connection he mentions Totte
ham as a particularly dark spot.) Goods in transit we
regularly pilfered on a large scale. Gangs operated. An
the streets of London and other large cities were infeste
with prostitutes, plying their trade with little let o
hindrance.

Sir Robert Peel's suggestion of a regular police for

'as at first met with hostility by many. They declared ıat 'police' was a French word and a French idea. 'hinking semantically, they said it augured ill. Probbly the police would be more of a nuisance and expense ıan the burglars. However, cooler counsels prevailed, nd the vital decision was taken to put an end to the ›rdid state of affairs. The point is that had that state of ffairs, almost incredible to the modern citizen of ,ondon, not existed, the situation as we know it today ıight never have come to pass.

It was but one instance of how progress works, at any ıte in England.

A far more comprehensive example is afforded by the hanging conditions which led, after many hesitations nd disappointments, to the Labour Party and T.U.C. – ›, in a word, the institution of Transport House. For it is possible for an Englishman of the present day to nvisage the absence of a police force, it would require far more strenuous feat of the imagination to conceive ıe country without Transport House. Yet there were, f course, many centuries when such was, indeed, the ase.

The records show that at one time, and over a long retch of time, the most common type of person in ngland was a peasant. In the parlance of the period ıey were known, collectively, as 'the peasantry'. Their atus – involving villeinage, the glebe, Lollards and the ke – is both too familiar and too complex to require or e susceptible of elucidation here. Suffice it to say that in ıose more leisurely and perhaps more truly thoughtful

days, before a profusion of cheap literature was avail
able to all, everyone knew a peasant when he saw one
and could talk intelligently about the peasantry.

And the peasantry, on its side, got itself, as the sayin
goes, 'talked about' by means of the various 'peasan
revolts' which bore such a colourful feature of th
period.

'Can you hear something rattling?'

Some historians have rashly assumed that 'th
peasantry' may be regarded as simply the Labou
Party and T.U.C. in embryo. It is pointed out that the
formed unions, and made a special point of resistin
attempts by the Government to 'freeze' wages, despi

he obvious effect of such attempts upon the inflationary spiral which followed the Black Death.

The analysis is superficial and will hardly bear :xamination. To take but one example, they hated awyers, and killed or severely beat many of that pro-ession who, properly approached, might have been of great service to the Movement. Moreover by per-nitting, if not actually encouraging, the murder of the Archbishop of Canterbury, Wat Tyler would certainly ave rendered himself ineligible for membership of any :onstituency Party.

The Peasant period proper thus ended in comparative ailure, and, for a while, people's attention concentrated on the Elizabethan Age and all that it implied. But with he coming of the Civil War, the Parliamentarians and he Roundheads, including Levellers, Diggers (early :rypto-anarchists), and the like, the question again arose whether we did not have here the germ, to put it no higher, of an incipient Labour Party. There were, or example, dissensions and divergences of view. And a man like John Lilburne might be thought likely to nake his mark in the Movement. He had close connec-ions with the Law, and on reaching the rank of Colonel n the Army resigned, on a political point, and sued the War Office for a considerable sum of money. He also wrote copiously for the Press.

Unfortunately his language was intemperate and nuch of his satire unconstructive. Many level-headed back-benchers were disgusted, and although after everal terms of imprisonment he became a Quaker, he did not have the full confidence of the level-headed

The fact was that, not for the first or last time, th
over-zealous attitude of certain elements had alienate
the middle-class voter. For more than a hundred year
it began to look as though progress had stopped. An
this was particularly the case because, just as the middle
class vote was getting over its fright, the whole advanc
was set back by the ill-judged behaviour of the smal
group of extremists responsible for the French Revo
lution with its repugnant excesses. Hot-heads i
England did the cause what might have been irrepar
able harm by forming Societies and Associations – wit
names like the Friends of the People – which expresse
more or less open sympathy with the Jacobins an
alienated the middle-class vote all over again. To smas
the panels of the King's coach in the streets of London
and organize a mutiny at the Nore was no way t
convince the country of the Movement's innate sense c
responsibility.

Half a century later, the Chartists – many of whon
were indeed men with a very, very deep sense of respon
sibility – permitted themselves to be infiltrated by wha
have been called 'crypto-embryo-communists', with th
inevitably alienating effect upon the sound men. Only
couple of decades later, Karl Marx made a typicall
malign attempt to discredit the English Labou
Movement by deliberately associating himself with i
and attempting to play a major role in its foundation.

Fortunately, the common sense of Englishmen a
length detected him as theorist and doctrinaire,

harge from which he was never able to clear himself.

Yet, despite all these threats to its birth and progress – lespite the 'Cloth-Cap Deviation' and the 'Tony 'andy Error' – Transport House was eventually born. and from that point on the student may trace the course f progress with a clear and steady hand.

XVII

THE ENGLISH MIND

Pre-frontal

IDESPREAD DISAGREEMENT and du biety shroud the question of the exac date at which what has been loosel termed 'psychology' first appeared i England. It is, however, safe to say tha in this, as indeed in every other investi gation, extreme views, obviously absurd and clearl inconsonant with the facts, are best avoided. They ca cause nothing but trouble. The statement (often littl better than a vague notion) that it was smuggled int England from Vienna during the first decade of th present century and helped to cause the *malaise* whic brought about the first World War is not only not quit true, but quite untrue, and founded, to boot, on a mis conception due to a confusion of psychology, in it richest and widest sense, with mere psycho-analysis. T assert, on the other hand, that Shakespeare read a chea manual on the Oedipus complex before writing *Haml* is also false. No such manual existed at the time. Thi fact alone is enough to explain why Shakespeare, an many another, did not know what he was talking about

This should not, notwithstanding, be taken to mea that everyone prior to – to make an arbitrary divisio which probably would not bear more than a very distant scrutiny – April 1913, was thoughtless. On the contrary, research shows that even quite early Englishmen, and even one or two women who became noted for the practice, thought a good deal. They were, of course, usually wrong, and their most cherished beliefs were going to turn out to be fallacies. But since they had no means of knowing this, they were none the worse, and sometimes better off. Many of them could put a fallacy to almost as good use as an ascertained twentieth-century truth.

Thus a man in a London tavern (it must be remembered that this was before the coffee-house was opened as a resort for wits, gallants, oglers and other components of the population as it came to exist in the eighteenth century) remarked in agitation to his companion of the hour – it was 11.15 on the evening of Thursday, 2nd August, 1492 – that after giving the matter some careful consideration he had come to the conclusion that 'this fellow Christopher Columbus, due to set sail tomorrow from southern Spain in the expectation of getting straight to India by sailing westwards across the Atlantic ocean, is basing his whole plan on a fallacy. Suppose there's something – not necessarily America, mind you, but just *something* – in the way, which I think there almost certainly is?'

Fortunately the companion of the hour was a man of sturdy common sense who had recently seen through the claims of the impostor Lambert Simnel, and was shortly going to see through those of the impostor Perkin Warbeck, too.

He replied, with a sagacity which even people pro
perly equipped with modern thought-aids might hav
envied, 'Makes no real difference; if something isn'
there, something else will be. He can't lose.'

Some years later, when many younger folk wer
already taking the discovery of America for granted
and even laughing about it in an ill-bred manner which
caused several people to turn and ask sharply: 'I
nothing sacred?', the man who had passed the origina
remark about the fallacy underlying Columbus's calcu
lations happened to encounter the other man as the
both were edging their way to the bar during the inter
val at a bear-baiting. (Time had, ineluctably, movec
on and the hour was now 3.15 on the afternoon o
2nd August, 1502.)

This, as will be recalled by those who have reac
earlier chapters, was the year when the Dutch intro
duced gardening, in the modern sense, to England. The
court of Star Chamber had already been in existence for
sixteen years, and the two friends were indeed glad to
see one another in such excellent health and fettle. One
(it is not difficult to guess which) remarked that in his
opinion a great deal of what passed for horticulture wa
based on a fallacy; he could not, he said, see anything
much being accomplished until gardeners were provided
with some good chemical weed-killer, not currently available due to the limited scientific resources of the very early
sixteenth century. He added, for good measure, that in
his judgment, for what it was worth, the court of Star
Chamber was based on some kind of fallacy, too.

'Mark my words,' said he, 'sooner or later that set-up is going to be exposed; its arbitrary interference with the freedom of the individual, with the Englishman's inalienable right to a fair trial with no holds barred, and, furthermore, with his right to be warned that anything he says near the beginning of the whole sordid business *will* be taken down and *may* be used in evidence against him ('I am', said he in a parenthesis which he did not attempt to disguise, 'something of a stickler for getting that so often misquoted phrase right') will be shown up as foredoomed to ultimate and ignominious failure. Don't you think so?'

'Could be, or not,' replied the other, with a certain caution, for he had retained his sturdy common sense and it told him that chances were that this old friend had taken gainful civil-service employment as a *provocateur*, ready to sell his pal for a butt of malmsey.

His interlocutor, who had insisted on treating him to a double sack, showed no offence at the ambivalence.

'You recall', he pursued, 'our last meeting, when I was worried about that fallacy Columbus had? Well only this morning I was thrilled by the realization that in point of fact both of us were right – I because I said his idea about where India was was fallacious, which by Henry it was, and you because you said it didn't really matter, and now look what's happened.'

'Absolutely,' assented his *vis-à-vis* with alacrity, and, feeling that the conversation had now been steered into safer channels, spoke at length on significant developments in the history of the mariner's compass, which at that time was being freely discussed wherever men met for the purpose.

'Is it not', he said, 'almost *bizarre* to reflect that in the sixty-fourth year of the reign of Hwang-ti, 2634 B.C., the Chinese emperor Hiuan-yuan, also called Hwang-Ti, attacked one Tchi-yeou on the plains of Tchou-lou, and, finding his army embarrassed by a thick fog raised by the enemy, constructed a chariot, Tchi-nan, for indicating the south, so as to distinguish the four cardinal points, and was thus enabled to pursue Tchi-yeou and take him prisoner, Honestly,' he said, chuckling appreciatively, 'you can't beat the Chinese, can you? Chariot to indicate the south! Makes me smile every time I think of it. Nothing new under the sun sort of business I mean to say, what?'

But his fellow bear-bait-viewer was not encouraging. 'Your undiscriminating admiration for, admittedly, a great people is,' he said, 'in this respect based, I am sorry to tell you, on a fallacy. The account which you seem to have accepted *au pied de la lettre* is purely mythical. The earliest allusion to the power of the lodestone in Chinese literature occurs in a Chinese dictionary finished in A.D. 121 – mark that – wherein the lodestone is defined as 'a stone with which an attraction can be given to a needle', but this knowledge (as you must surely be aware) is no more than that existing in Europe at least five hundred years before. Chariots my foot! Excuse my sneer.'

Though neither man fully realised it, the controversy about how much to believe about China had begun.

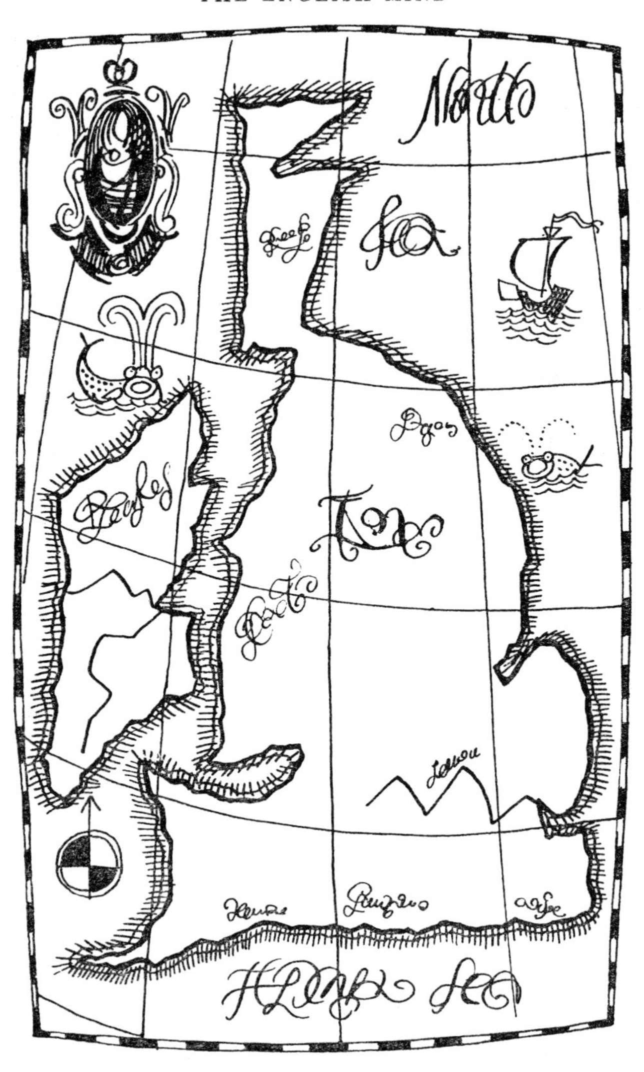

The episode serves to illustrate the point that even at that date, a full eighteen years before G. Lilly drew the first map of England (much of it, of course, inaccurate), Englishmen were exercising their inalienable right to express their opinions without fear or favour. A Spaniard of the period who had let himself become adjusted to absolutism was amazed.

'What's that you are exercising so late at night?' he queried of a passing Englishman.

'My inalienable right.' He was told, as the fellow countryman of John Bunyan, and later of John Wilkes, paused, under a lamp-post; 'of course I know it's a mongrel, but for my part I consider them almost invariably more intelligent than some of these over-bred specimens. May be wrong, Señor, but that's what I always say. Matter of personal opinion'.

'Caramba.'

'Quite.'

'It's dogged as does it,' an innocent by-stander (whom an old stand-by had asked to stand by) permitted himself to observe. He knew that he was seeing English character at its best. Furthermore, though innocent, he was dogged by a guilt feeling, *Angst* in the nastiest sense of the word.

Having *Angst* in the early sixteenth century was no joke at all. Not realising that everyone else had it too, people felt lonesome and unpleasantly unique. Extroverts – unwitting, naturally, of how extrovert they were – were jostling introverts at every corner saying, 'It's only something you ate. Probably that fish. Why not join one of these new, rebellious sects and cut out fish on Fridays? Do you a power of good.'

'I have always been given to understand,' riposted the man who had been jostled at the corner, with a good deal of dignity, 'that there were only two sexes. Which are these other ones that are in rebellion?'

'I said sects,' shouted the forward-looking reformer.

'I heard you the first time,' said the jostle-ee quietly, 'and personally I wish you would try to get the subject off your mind. After all, there are other things in life.'

'Such as?' parried his chance acquaintance of the minute.

'Well like as it might be madrigals or exploration,' hazarded chance acquaintance number Two.

Though neither of them was fully aware of it, the controversy about how much to believe about sex, sects and madrigals had begun.

(In this connection it should be mentioned that the G. Lilly mentioned above as having at least tried to draw the first map of England was not the same person as William Lilly (1602–1681), noted English astrologer, who spent a lot of the cavalier-roundhead period, which at first seemed to irk and bore him, reading Valentine Naibod's *Commentary on Alchabitius*. He found it excellent stuff, and said so. 'The profoundest author I ever met with' was his comment on the commentary.

This renewed his interest in politics and from then on, according to himself, he 'did carefully take notice of every grand action betwixt king and parliament, and did first then incline to believe that as all sublunary affairs depend on superior causes, so there was a possibility of discovering them by the configurations of the superior bodies'.

The practice of making a little something out of what the stars foretell had begun.

A book about William Lilly says, among other comments on his way of life, that he 'lived on friendly and almost intimate terms with Bulstrode Whitlock, Lenthall the Speaker, Sir Philip Stapledon, Elias Ashmole and others'. (One would have supposed that with such a stable of friends he would hardly have needed 'others', but some men are like that.)

Another book, and it is, when all's said and done, no less than the *Encyclopaedia Britannica*, takes a very grudging, not to say snide, attitude to Lilly, remarking for a start that 'even Selden seems to have given him some countenance'. 'Even' in this context is a bad word. And research shows that Selden himself had no good cause to adopt this patronising attitude and then go down to posterity in it. It was in bad taste, and showed a lack of consideration for Lilly's family and circle of more intimate friends.

'Probably,' babbles the Encyclopaedia, in an all too common access of character assassination, 'the chief difference between him' (it's the same Willy we speak of, God rest his great soul) 'and the mass of the community at the time was that while others' – How many others? Are their birth-certificates available? – 'believed in the general truth of astrology, he ventured to specify the future events to which its calculations pointed'. (How in heaven's name he could have earned any money if he had not so ventured, the Encyclopaedia man does not 'venture to specify'. Nobody was going to pay out a piece of eight for the news, in 1650 or thereabouts, that 'political conditions are likely to be disturbed towards the end of the week but a merry heart goes all the way'. What they wanted to know, and what this Lilly was trying to tell them, was who was going to win the civil war, and put their shirts on it.

'Even', says the smear-man in the big-book, 'from his own account of himself, it is evident that he did not trust implicitly to the indications given by the heavens, but like more vulgar fortune-tellers' (and if ever a libel was committed that is one) 'kept his eyes and ears open for any information which might make his predictions safe. It appears that he had correspondents both at home and in foreign parts to keep him conversant with the probable current of affairs.'

Journalism, in other words, had begun. And the decent-minded folk who through the ages have formed so large a percentage of the English population will note with a certain disgust that the man is first somewhat jeered at for believing that stars foretell, and then given a dirty look for not keeping this belief 'implicit' and having, as a stand-by, his Own Correspondents. No wonder that the unhappy Lilly moved to Surrey, dropped astrology, became a doctor instead and died, spurned by Charles II for not foreseeing the Restoration.

Reverting, as in history one often must, to the guilty-feeling innocent by-stander whose part in Anglo-

Spanish relations proved so disappointingly insignificant, the reader will recall that, when last seen he was letting *Angst*, like a bug in a petal, feed on his damask cheek. Specifically his trouble was that here was the fifteenth century, with all its very very real meaning, going round the bend into the sixteenth century and *its* tremendous significance, and he had hardly noticed what was happening.

They said to him: 'What did you really feel, Max – you don't mind my calling you Max, do you? I feel we've known each other since, well ha-ha, the fifteenth century – about that time when you had Henry VII there and the whole while you knew that in a scant seven years Henry VIII was coming up? Would you care to tell us something about that? I'm sure everyone else is just as interested as I am in what must have been quite - ha-ha - well quite an experience, eh Max?'

'Certainly was.'

'Care to expatiate?'

'Well, I know things are different nowadays but the fact is it all seemed sort of, sort of, sort of . . .'

'Natural, would you say, at the time?'

'Yus.'

'Well, thank you very much indeed, Mr Bystander, or may I say Max, and I'm sure everyone's been just as interested as I have. I'm sure nobody's been less so, ha-ha.'

It was with the idea of meeting just this sort of problem – *Angst*, Guilt, the whole lot – that Freud, Jung, Adler and others (all excellent but too numerous for individual mention), set up their psych-business at about the time they did. At first people laughed at their claim to be able to take anything off people's minds that was on them, but later, not. Sigmund ('Mr Complex') Freud was soon seen everywhere, and it was generally recognized that in getting the English interested in sex he had done, as Baden-Powell is reported to have said, 'a good job of work'.

'B-P,' as he was affectionately known locally, further pointed out that whereas, previously, scouts, and others, had looked with incomprehension at the thing on their knives for getting stones out of horses' hooves, now, in the light of Freudian teaching, they had a pretty shrewd notion of what it all meant. 'Khaki' Roberts heartily concurred, 'though, mark my words,' he is alleged to have said, 'I don't go the whole way with Sigmund. Some of his stuff looks to me very much as though it were based on a fallacy'.

In the 1920's and 30's, Freudian Englishmen of the Old School were congratulating themselves on having what they rightly saw as a 'hey-day'. Like so many hey-days which may be called to mind, it was brief. Wiser counsels prevailed. Under the relentless pressure of new theories ever thrusting westwards, Freudians, first as single spies, later at battalion strength, started to emigrate to the United States. Manhattan, bought from the natives for a piece of psychiatric wampum, was first colonized, and it was not long before the intrepid but ruthless Id was advancing towards the heart of Chicago. And with an alacrity which the original Major Quisling,

O.B.E., might have envied, even college Presidents were soon surrendering to the invader, their imaginations fascinated and their previously rugged vitality sapped by a luxury of thought such as had never before been seen on their wind-swept homesteads. America had started contemplating its psychological navel with consequences which were to prove, in the fullness of time, of some importance.

Weakened by these defections, in England the sect was already tending to lose its identity. The libido was on the way out, and it was realized that, despite wild rumours of its behaviour, grossly exaggerated in the Sunday newspapers, which caused several people to turn and ask sharply 'Is nothing sacred?', the whole business was merely the product of natural high spirits and an inevitable disillusion brought on by contemplation of the Generals responsible for the battle of Passchendaele, the general strike and the general situation. No real harm had been done and there were no after-effects which a stiff dose of any good wonder-drug, preferably in the big economy-size packet, could not cure.

The complex, in other words, was yielding to the cortex. Despite the belated efforts of Jung-men to attract the interest of young men, more and more Englishmen began to feel that better results could be obtained by getting people down on the operating table and cutting the bad bit out of the brain-cortices by prefrontal leucotomy than by simply getting them down on the psychiatrist's couch.

'Just let me saw open that head and get the forceps on the cortex,' a practitioner of the new school observed, 'and old Sigmund can go chase his Ego round his super-Ego'.

Providence (almost always, as experience shows, on the right side) accelerated the development by developing the second World War. Cases of shell-shock, hitherto treated almost timorously, were now knocked down, intoxicated with ether, driven into screaming spasms and thus cured. No one who had been through 'the treatment' wanted that to happen again, and soon the streets of London town were full of gaily-caparisoned men jostling one another and remarking that in case anyone thought they ought to see a doctor, they just simply wanted to remark that being nearly burned alive in a tank had, to their minds, been an experience both amusing and exhilarating.

Nevertheless, in the plenitude of modern economy, there was enough for all. In Harley Street, where post-Pavlov men had long since become used to the bewildering luxury of Freudian civilization – they had stopped, after a time, putting coals in the bath and pulling the lavatory plug for fun, their slightly Mongolian features distorted by a mixture of emotions in which glee and awe were mingled –, the steady hum of the electrical machines curing all-comers of everything with a series of one-thousand-volt shocks bore witness to a basic prosperity belying foreign lies about the state of England.

It had been a long way from Boadicea, but England had made it.

XVIII

THE BUBBLE

'A real good time while it lasted' – Law

AN AMERICAN CRITIC, A. DENIZEN, of Wall Street, has recently described the English attitude to finance as 'over-cautious'. The statement betrays a degree of superficiality, ignorance and downright *insouciance* shocking in a scholar of this *provenance*. It is only too evident that he has not heard of the South Sea Bubble. Yet speak to an Englishman of finance, and it is to the SSB that his thoughts immediately fly. It is indeed almost the only event in English financial history which everyone has heard a little something about. And none of what has been heard is good.

Those who seek to prove that the South Sea Bubble was not so black as it has been painted are for the most part post-Keynesians, taking the general view that the more money there is about (however valueless it may appear in the jaundiced eyes of old-fashioned men at the Treasury and others who lack the *verve* and *élan* desirable in those who set out to push economics off their beachhead before Christmas), the (on the whole, and with all suitable qualifications) better.

'You mean,' the late Earl Balfour said tentatively to

Montague Norman, who tentatively passed the question on to Keynes, 'let everything rip?'

At the epoch in question, Keynes had just been made a Trustee of *The Times*, with the idea that he and an Archbishop and others of that kidney, would at least do their best to stop anything Gadarene happening in Printing House Square. Busy – and happy in his work – he was unable to come to the telephone at once to answer '64-dollar Balfour's' perfectly civil question, but gave a firm promise that in 'the long run' he would write a little volume on the subject which might easily make history, mark a turning point, give people to think. He had done it before, and he saw no reason why he should not do it again, and again and again and again. Incidentally, he was the first Englishman since

Horace Walpole to tell The Long Run to go jump in a lake. 'In the long run,' said Maynard Keynes, irked by a posse of dons who kept proving that whatever anyone did, nothing much was ultimately going to come of it, 'in the long run we are all dead'.

'Imagine saying a thing like that!' the man then heading the Treasury is reported to have remarked to the man then heading Barclay's Bank. 'It isn't very nice, is it?'

'Brilliant, but', said the Barclay chief, 'I'd say unsound.'

'You can say it again for me' muttered the watch-dog of England's finances.

'Mad I grant you, genius I don't say' was the remark contributed to the discussion by an economist from Cambridge, who by reason of his small intellectual stature had often been the butt of Keynes's teasing and even of jokes in the worst possible taste which gave him an inferiority complex that left him lurching helplessly from Marx to Pigou trying, ineffectively, to get his own back. It was not until the economist shortage of 1943 that he was able to find any sort of general acceptance by a public hungering for statistics and prepared to pay for almost any sort of graph provided it did not positively stink, and was firm enough to carry home in newspaper without slipping between the fingers. In many quarters it was cogently argued that the mere sight of him on the job, in charge of quite a sector of the nation's life, was enough to bring home to people the true meaning of the war. His subsequent elevation to the peerage, though opposed by some, was justified on the ground that it brought home to many thoughtless people the true meaning of the House of Lords.

He was, it need hardly be said, a stern and uncompromising opponent of the South Sea Bubble. Nothing, he was wont to say, that he had read written in praise of it had sufficed to alter his opinion that it was thoroughly disreputable, and quite unsuited to decently nurtured English men and women.

He may have been right. He may, on the other hand, have been wrong. And as students of the semantic, or linguistic-analytic, approach to history will be well aware, even these statements are examples of a naturalistic fallacy because – in the pungent words of an exponent – 'from is no must', meaning that the moment you lay so much as a moral paw on the factual 'is' and start in with your 'rights' and 'wrongs' and judgments of that type, you may as well pick up your cards and cease seeking employment in any of the better-sited history factories. It is a situation which ensures a lot more room at the top.

About the South Sea Bubble, however, there is this to be said: many an Englishman, depressed by the realization that he has given all his money to Horatio Bottomley, Ivar Krueger, or some Germans who needed it to buy tanks with and later went bankrupt with effects so beneficial to themselves that, freed of any obligation to pay anything on the original investment, they were excellently placed to push any Englishman they saw out of the Argentine, Rhodesia, and/or the

Bight of Benin, has thought back on the SSB and said to himself, with a little lift of the heart, a small twist of the upper lip: 'Leastways, brother, you're no more a bloody fool nor what they used to was.'

And with that thought, eyes sparkle again, beautiful women come flooding back, and a Geiger counter proving that a thousand pounds handed now, without a moment's delay, to a man whose address is Poste Restante, Edmonton, Alberta, will treble itself before you can say international nickel, looks very very good indeed.

A curious feature – it has become a collectors' item – of the SSB was that several of the Cabinet Ministers and other highly placed characters who had collaborated to rob the public of all but the last shilling stuck in the toe of the sock were actually arrested. One was put in the Tower for quite a while. Several men of business, displaying a nervous sensibility which would have been more acceptable in some other profession, cut their throats. Such doings, it need hardly be said, were not conducive to the growth of public confidence. Wild voices were raised in ill-considered denunciation of what was intemperately termed the 'wholesale corruption' of statesmen and officials. The phrase was, at the best, a loose one. Much of the merchandising was done retail, and in at least one case a man who was selling a Minister to a speculator found himself confronted with a crippling demand for 25 per cent sales tax. He called off the deal. Attacks on private enterprise, he pointed out, had begun.

As a result of this type of interfence, many men who earlier would have 'gone all-out' on bribe-collecting drives, confident that anything they could raise they could keep, became nervous, refused to take risks and thus missed golden opportunities. They were deflated, and knew it. It became difficult for up-and-coming men with a real faith in the future to sell a Bishop a sound deal in simony. The Englishman's belief that you ought to get plenty for damn little had received a rude blow.

XIX

PLAYING UP

'Give archery a fair deal!' says King

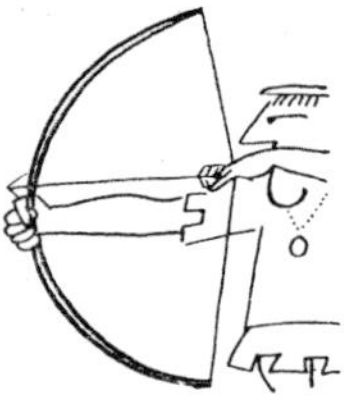

CRAZY DOINGS with big balls' (*rageries de grosses pelotes*) was how Edward II permitted himself to describe football a minute or two before signing a decree prohibiting it. Lovers of the game took some comfort from the fact that Edward was drunk when he did it, and sexually off the beam to boot, the principal object of his affections being none other than the notorious Piers Gaveston. As Mrs Markham, in her invaluable *History of England*, rightly says, it was 'a period of nearly twenty years of public disgrace and private calamity'.

It is true that not long after his attack on football – there is small doubt that it was he who urged the King to his intemperate action – Gaveston suffered the supreme indignity of having his head sawn off by an employee of the Earl of Lancaster. 'When the King', says Mrs Markham, 'heard of the death of his favourite he was thrown into agonies of grief . . . but he had not the power to make his resentment felt'.

A typical non-footballer (Macaulay, used privately to dub him 'the cissiest of English kings'), his notion of how to deal with the situation was to get another favourite alled Hugh Spenser. He must have known, as Mrs Markham later did, that this Spenser was 'a man of an nsolent temper and a rapacious disposition'. Not the ype, it was generally felt, for a favourite. Remarking vith a shrug that she supposed it 'takes all sorts to make world', Edward's wife Isabella, daughter of Philip the air, made arrangements to have the king jailed and leposed. He fainted when Judge Trussel, who said (as o many have said before and since) that he was speak- ng in the name of the English people, brought him he news that he had stopped being king in all but ame.

Not content with that, they ordered him to be shaved vith dirty ditch-water. The king burst into tears and nade a *mot.* 'Here', said he, referring to the tears then treaming down his bristly cheeks, 'is clean warm water vhether you will or no.' Soon afterwards they murdered im. Then, on account of the scant attention paid to ublic nutrition while all this was going on, there was a amine. Robbery with violence was also practised on a arge scale. 'If they had only let them go on playing ootball' remarked a contemporary thinker 'none of his would have happened.'

Edward's alleged reason for his high-handed action – ypically, neither he nor Gaveston knew whether it was occer or rugger that they were prohibiting – was that eople playing football in the streets of London (many of them apprentices trying to get in some jostling ractice) made such a noise that people could not get wink of sleep. And it is true that in the fourteenth century Wembley was but a bold, imaginative idea. Nor were pools properly organized.

For reasons which nobody has so far been able to ascertain, football was played everywhere, from the Tower to the Elephant, more on Shrove Tuesday than on any other day. Yet since Easter was already a movable feast, taking the whole of Lent, Ash Wednesday, Good Friday and, naturally, Shrove Tuesday, together with many another well known date, hither and yon with it, the question of how the fixtures were fixed remains just what it has been described as, namely a question.

Although Edward II was the first English king to become really frightened of football, he was by no means the last. In those days almost everyone was scared of it. Edward III, though he had achieved the not very difficult task of being a better man than his father, still could not stand the noise. But, showing a political shrewdness which had entirely eluded Gaveston, he claimed that he was only anti-footer because he was pro-archery. He said that people were stopping shooting arrows and shooting balls instead.

A man about the court (not, it must in all fairness, be said at once, a favourite man), said 'Why not just simply sign a decree, saying football must stop?'

To this the monarch, after stating for the record 'you are not my favourite man', not unreasonably riposted that he thought his father had signed that decree years ago, and why did he have to do it all over again? Otiose was a word he used.

'Can't we' he pleaded 'ban football for good, or are –

to take couple of names at random – Henry VIII and glorious Gloriana going, in the fullness of time, to have to keep signing this damned anti-ball decree? Balls, indeed!' he added thoughtfully.

'It may', interposed the venerable Lord Chamberlain with dignity, 'be all b . . ls to you, your Majesty, but a lot of these apprentices think it's the coming game.'

'When I say a thing's balls, it's b . . ls' shouted the king, 'and in that statement I include hockey and even lacrosse, which may be introduced from Canada any time now.'

He banned it again, and, as he had foreseen, Henry VIII and Queen Elizabeth did it too. Sir Thomas Elyot had a word or two to say about the game, summing up, in 1531, what seems to have been the general view. 'Football', he wrote, 'is nothing but beastly fury and extreme violence, whereof proceedeth hurt and consequently rancour and malice to remain with them that be wounded.'

'Elyot hits out at soccer racket' was the headline they put on his statement.

James I, with a typical mixture of egotism and political acumen, let the masses get on with it but forbade Charles I, then a mere lad, to play it, saying that all anyone could get out of that game was a crippled leg. It has been argued that had Charles I been allowed to indulge in the sport like normal boys – is our Prince being molly-coddled? was a question on many people's lips – he might have been better fitted to meet, in later life, people of normal upbringing like Pym, Cromwell and the leaders of the East Anglian League.

It may well be so, in which case the course of English history would, of course, have suffered a definite change of course.

Asked for his estimate of these possibilities, the Manager of a well known football Club, not a thousand miles from either Manchester or Newcastle (a position which permitted many gate-crashers to get into the act), said 'of course'.

A thing which caused a good deal of worry to the 'fans' – later to be termed 'hip-cats' – of fifteenth-century football was that women kept playing it too. Seeing them there, barging, dribbling and tackling up and down Westminster Bridge and the Strand, anyone might have taken them for Russians. It made Gaveston turn in his grave.

Sex-equality was coming in. It had to go out and rest a while, but later, headed by George Eliot, a number of Brontës, and Florence Nightingale, it returned with a song in its heart. And it has stayed with us ever since, sometimes, it is true, in the attic, but that was only when there was that trouble with the plumbing, and always a very dear and highly valued visitor.

The English Rugby Union was founded in 1871.

Unknown to later women, who supposed themselves to be doing something new, early thirteenth-century women played cricket, and seem to have seen some sort of sexual significance in what, as a contemporary man pointed out to them, had been intended as an essentially healthy pastime.

The idea of a lot of sexy women playing cricket –

Hondyn or Greag' as it was called at the time – was
ıaturally repugnant to Piers Gaveston no less than to
Hugh Spenser, and they urged the king to suppress it.
In a rare moment of stubbornness, and realizing that a
ing who stops cricket is not going to remain king for
ong, Edward II refused.

'Oh if that's the way you feel, Eddie,' said Gaveston,
louncing, 'I don't suppose there's anything more to be
aid except that I'm never, never, never going to feel
uite the same about *you* ever again. I thought this
ntire court was under the influence of a certain type of
ndividual. Couldn't get anywhere, they always gave
ne to understand, unless you were one of "them".'

'What you've been and gone and done, Piers,' said Edward, 'is to make an intelligible but quite possibly disastrous confusion between "queens" in your sense of the word, and The Queen. Oh hullo Isabella, we were just chatting about this and that. How's your father, Philip the Fair?'

The toiling masses (it must be remembered that there was no Labour Party in those days) soldiered on with their cricket, although Edward III, as usual, said that it was a 'dishonest game, absolutely useless and cowardly' because it kept people away from archery – the trouble people had with their archery-practice in those days should serve to remind some contemporary citizens that others have suffered in the past from inconveniences just as bad as having to turn out on a Sunday morning to handle an atomic warhead.

Edward IV, who was handsome, spent much of his time being vicious, and disregarded a timely warning from the Duke of Burgundy to the effect that things were not going too well, was, nevertheless, the first English king to put down in black and white that cricket was criminal, and that anyone who played it was going to be locked up for two years, pay a fine of £10 and have his bat, bails and ball burned.

'We seem', observed a sagacious contemporary, a keen student of the sport, 'to be on a rather sticky wicket'.

A man charged under the Act with playing the game was, however, able to argue successfully that 'it wasn't cricket', thus originating the phrase.

The fourth Earl of Salisbury was, however, the 'resident, in 1661, of the St Albans Cricket Club, dis- laying once again the famous capacity of the Cecil amily for making friends and influencing people. It was George II who finally gave up the unequal struggle, aying that English people could play cricket provided hey never bet more than £10 on the outcome of a given ame. Three years later a cricket ball struck the Prince f Wales in the stomach and killed him. It was, how- ver, deemed too late to reverse the course of action dopted by the Crown. General regret was, nevertheless, xpressed – some of it immediately, and more later, hen there had been time to assess George III. To this xtent it is correct to say that cricket caused the loss of he American colonies.

Logating and shove-groat were other pastimes to hich Englishmen were addicted, and there was a con- derable body of opinion in favour of permitting them indulge freely in these pleasures. Sterner counsels, owever, prevailed. There was only one objection to ich games, but it was a decisive one – they interfered ith archery. Henry VIII got a report showing that as consequence of the growing indifference to archery sulting from the popularity of – for instance – shove- roat, bow and arrow manufacturers were finding it ifficult to sell their product and were emigrating to cotland, 'to the great comfort of strangers and etriment of this realm'. The king, who had only just ot over his annoyance at the number of under-sized orses in the country, was furious and took drastic

action to stop anyone doing almost anything in thei
spare time except shoot arrows from bows.

Betting was on the prohibited list, so that it can b
seen that the English anti-betting laws which have fron
time to time brought a puzzled smile to the lips of th
foreigner did not originate, as was once supposed, wit
spoil-sport Puritans, but were designed to save archery
As so often happens in history, archery was after all no
saved on any significant scale, but nobody saw fit t
repeal the betting laws on that account. It is an axion
of good English Government that you should neve
repeal a law, regulation or tax until you are perfectl
sure that you have at least one other law, regulation c
tax to put in its place. The Government which allow
itself to run out of legislation is not acting responsibly.

XX

THE GENTLE READER

A trot round the heart of men and things

N VIEW OF the finely significant role played in English history by the English press – had it indeed not been for the vigour and vigilance of the press, much of English history might almost as well not have happened at all for all the attention it would have attracted – it is unfortunate (since the fact can and has been used as the raw material of ill-natured jokes by foreigners and other unscrupulous critics) that the first regular English newspaper, the *English Mercurie* of 1588, copies of which are preserved in the British Museum, is not a regular English newspaper published in 1588 at all but a forgery done in the mid-eighteenth century, shortly before he became the 2nd Earl of Hardwicke, by the individual who was later to become the 2nd Earl of Hardwicke.

Englishmen with the interests of public opinion at heart did their best, in private conversation, to dissuade the Earl-to-be (living, at the time, under the name of Philip Yorke, Yorke chancing to be, in fact, his family name) from a project which might all too easily bring what was soon to be termed 'the Fourth Estate' into bad odour. There is, it is true, no record of these conversations, a fact which underlines their authenticity, since, being private, to have them on public record would be a distinctly suspicious circumstance. In any case no doubt about them can be entertained. There have always been, and it is a matter for strong national self-congratulation, English men ready and willing to dissuade anyone from doing or saying anything of which they could not themselves immediately see the point.

'But what's the point, Philip, old man?' a fellow Fellow of the Royal Society said to him in 1744, when both of them were visiting Reigate, M.P. for which Yorke at the time was. The battle of Dettingen was by now little more than a memory of the good time England had had last year, and Culloden was in the womb of the future.

'Thought it might be rather amusing' laughed Yorke in mingled mischief and *insouciance*. (He had for some time been publishing an *insouciant jeu d'esprit* entitled *The Athenian Letters*, which purported to be an English translation of letters written, during the Peloponnesian war, when Pericles and Alcibiades, to name but two, were prominent, by a Persian secret service man working in Athens, and their success may have gone to his head. Some people actually believed that they really were an English translation of a Spanish translation of a fifth-century-B.C. Persian document because, they reasoned, why would anyone trouble to make up a thing like that? In so reasoning they had seriously miscalculated the man Yorke.)

'But look here,' exclaimed the other, 'suppose people

believe this *Mercurie* thing really is, I mean was, the first English newspaper?'

'They will,' said Yorke, 'that's the joke'.

'Is nothing sacred?' cried his erstwhile friend, as he left Reigate in a dudgeon so high that it was seen for miles around and taken, by the superstitious, as a sign that at an early date the Young Pretender was going to land in Scotland and seek to march on London before anyone had had time to put into final form the words and music of *God Save the King* or to settle controversies about its origin. In the event, the Jacobites were foiled, and in 1745 its performance was already *de rigueur* at Covent Garden. It was a favourite of the Duke of Cumberland who hummed it throughout his successful campaign. Its popularity thus assured, the French claimed that one of their countrymen had written the tune, and the Germans, more practical and *schrecklich*, made arrangements to smuggle it to Berlin where for years it was used as, of all things, the German national anthem, thinly disguised under the words *Heil Dir im Siegerkranz*.

Only the enforced abdication of Kaiser Wilhelm II in 1918 put an end to the practice.

Although, by reason of Philip Yorke's wry, and, as some may think, perverted sense of humour, people in 1588 who wanted to subscribe to a regular newspaper had to wait more than 150 years and then make do with an impudent forgery, journalists and public alike maintained their determination to have an English press at all costs – which was fortunate in view of how high the cost later proved to be.

The situation developed so favourably that by 1614 Richard ('Mr Blues') Burton, after seeing *The Anatomy of Melancholy* through the press (he declined to make personal appearances at leading marts to autograph the book on the ground that to do so would be 'undignified') was able to get on record as the first man to say that the reading-habit was dying out among the English and that if they read anything it was mostly trash – 'Sir Huon of Bordeaux, Amadis de Gaul etc., a playbook, or some pamphlet of news'.

A man called Williams F. Cudlipp, believed to have been a forebear of descendants of that name, asked Burton why the devil people should not read news pamphlets if they wanted to?

'Not everyone has to be so highbrow as you' he said indignantly. 'And anyway,' he added with a touch of heat, 'it keeps them out of the stews and bagnios of a Sunday morning.'

'But', protested Burton, amazed at such an attitude, 'a lot of their so-called information is not only "angled" for political motives, but grossly sensational. I was reading one the other day which was quite evidently trying to suggest that in a few decades there may well be a civil war in this country. I ask you! Those fellows, mark my words, are half of them foreigners, with no deep understanding of the English character. Civil war, indeed! Here! We aren't living in the Wars of the Roses!'

'I'm willing to admit,' said Williams F. Cudlipp, 'that that series on Henry VIII and His Loves – what did they call it? "Blood on the Bedspread" or something of the kind – sailed a bit close to the wind, but, after all, it's surely a good thing for people to have their interest in their country's history stimulated, even though it may be done by methods which would, perhaps, not win the unqualified approval of an old fuddy-duddy like our friend Archbishop Laud.'

'Oh well,' retorted Burton, 'if you're going to use that sort of argument this discussion could go on for ever.'

'More than 340 years, so far as I can see', agreed Williams F. Cudlipp, making a rapid mental calculation. And he was right, showing that when it comes to accuracy there are few to equal the English journalist. That this was no flash in the pan is indicated by the fact that several of his descendants, if such indeed they were, lived to edit important newspapers and put things in proper perspective.

Newspaper editors of the sixteenth (though at that time they were more in the nature of News Letters – 'just Fuggering about' as one, more cynical than the rest, was wont to express it), seventeenth and eighteenth centuries loved the life, but agreed it was apt to give a man ulcers.

If he was against the Government, he was suppressed, ruined by unjust penalties and exactions, or jailed. Often enough all three happened to him in the course of a single afternoon. This made it extraordinarily hard for him to be as objective as, he well knew, the traditions of English journalism demand that an editor must be. His evaluations would get blurred and he would be criticized for allowing what was essentially comment to creep into the news columns.

On the other hand, should he lend the Government his support, people were going to say that he was a sycophant, hired-hack, toady, and lick-spittle. 'Sold his pen for gold,' they would remark with a supercilious shrug, 'and we thought he was sincere all that time when he used to spiel about the Common People. Ah well, I have seen four-and-thirty leaders of revolts. Handful of silver sort of business, I suppose.'

Particularly annoying was the fact that many of these men on the Government side had the utmost difficulty in collecting the pay they got from the secret funds – 'the rate for the jobbery' as it was currently called.

'It's gotten so', a contemporary of Defoe is reported to have said, 'that around here a man has to work as hard to get properly corrupted as if he were some kind of mangy independent.'

Others sought to climb out of the quandary by selling themselves in turn, and, in the case of energetic journalists determined to get ahead, simultaneously, to both sides. But a public for the most part grossly ignorant of the problems facing men seeking to carry on the functions of the press as the only guarantee of freedom, truth and justice as we know them, said 'turncoats', 'hired gladiators', 'awfully unreliable', 'cancel the order', and remarked what a pity it was that Defoe himself, who had admittedly written a really excellent and probably definitive book about Robinson Crusoe, should find it necessary to go about the country snooping, invading privacy, and in general demeaning himself by becoming involved in quite early journalism.

However, when things were darkest, there occurred, as so often happens in England, something really good. *The Times* was founded, and for a good many years it looked as though journalism had gone about as far as it could go. *The Times*, throughout the greater part of the nineteenth century fulfilled so many indispensable functions – apart from safeguarding truth, freedom and

decency and striking out at Parnell with a set of forgeries which made the late Hardwicke look like an amateur – that nobody could imagine how they had got on without it. Indeed much that had, from time to time, gone awry in English history was now explained, for before *The Times* became required reading at the Palace, Kings, Privy Counsellors and others quite sincerely engaged in trying to think what on earth to do for the best, were floundering in a morass of misinformation, much of it written by people of whom it was doubtful whether they were even gentlemen. They heard some rumour about a revolt at Kiev or wherever it might be, but there was no Special or Own Correspondent to put them straight on which was the right side, due ultimately to prevail, and which were the small bands of extremists, scheduled to lose public confidence any day now.

'Johnnie,' a man said to John Walter I just before this pioneer of genius was jailed and ruined, 'don't worry about anything. Seventy years or so from now, long after you're dead and gone, absolutely "top" people are all going to be reading *The Times*.'

'Well that's a comfort' Walter replied. 'But what's worrying me just at the minute, apart from this business of being a jailed bankrupt, is did I or did I not do right to change the title? You recall that when I first started the old rag in 1785, I called it *The London Daily Universal Register, printed logographically*. I liked that old title,' mused the victim of royal enmity, 'it had something. And then I got this hunch that what was needed was something snappier. I felt it all at once, here. And one night – I'd been dining with Pitt, as I recall, to explain the situation in France to him – it suddenly came to me. I would call it *The Times*, and in 1788, as you probably remember, I did so. Was I right, old man?'

'Johnnie,' the old man said, 'you were so damn right that not such a very long time after you're mouldering in the sod, your demise hastened, I should hardly wonder, by financial anxiety and political bitterness, people are going to start referring to it as The Thunderer. Kind of nice, eh?'

'Swell!' replied 'Johnnie' Walter with the quiet dignity which was already becoming the pre-requisite to employment in Printing House Square. ('We're all squares here' was a favourite boast of staff members in later days.)

It is, however, a well known thing about England, one, indeed, of those things which have kept the country in the same place for longer than was expected by many, that nothing really stands still for ever. Any report to the contrary is based on a crude optical illusion.

The future Lord Northcliffe, some years before he became the former Mr Harmsworth, had an idea – and although at the time many people said it was a bad one, it now is seen to have been, in however restricted a sense of the word, a 'good' one. It was (though, in the very late Victorian period with which he had to work, many commentators, shrinking from reality, urged that the term be banned as 'likely to corrupt' the mentality of men-about-town) nothing less than the *Daily Mail.*

Harmsworth as he was – Northcliffe to many a subsequent citizen – had fingers, and counted on them. If, said he – speaking mostly to himself, and tapping the table the while with a pencil to throw the built in-mikes off-balance – so-and-so many so-and-so's have been taught to read by the Education Acts, it stands to reason that not more than 9 per cent of them have been taught to read hard enough to snuggle up instantly with *The Times.* They could get repelled, and leave journalism altogether, turning instead to the bicycle, the kaleidoscope, the dissolving view, or morbid contemplation of the impending war in South Africa. As an Ulsterman he became depressed about the future of England and made up his mind to take a hand.

Among other things known about him, and very much to his credit, is the fact that (*a*) he made the lift-boy editor, in the broad interests of democracy (the story, being, one need hardly say, untrue, having been circulated by Northcliffe himself in the broad interests of democracy), (*b*) he asked one of the assistant Editors who was trying to punch his time-clock at the sack after being a little late at the hire, 'Why are a lot of people in Hampstead going to be walking about the Heath in top-hats today?'

The 'human-interest' story had begun.

The man, who needed the money, and hoped the hire would go on a little bit longer before the sack, had the common sense to say: 'Chief, I haven't any idea. Why, Chief! The things you know and think of, Chief! By the way, Chief, ever get the feeling one of your boots needs licking? Ring me any time.'

Kindly, generous, and ever ready to indulge another's whim, the Chief – later to be dubbed Lord Northcliffe – offered the man a kindly and generous boot-toe, and said 'Jews'.

'How so, Chief?' cried the near-editor from his stooping posture. 'Gee, Chief, you know everything. Dues? I'll join the Union today.'

'Not dues you oaf, Jews!' roared the Emperor of Fleet Street. 'Bedad, what's the use of the Education Acts if we get a situation of this character, which leaves me frankly nonplussed?'

''Tis but for the nonce, Chief', responded the loyal employee.

Harmsworth, who was using the name at the time claiming, correctly, that it was his own, said: 'Where was I?'

Disentangling his tongue from the lace – and, let the student note, in those days boots were boots, whereas nowadays a man licks a boot and it's low on the ground and might even be suède in which case the difference of before and after lick can hardly be noticed – the man currently in charge of moulding English opinion on Mr H's behalf said he thought, but was not prepared to state as an absolute fact, that the pair of them had been having some sort of discussion about Golders Green.

It was at this point that the Great Man showed his greatness. 'Yom', said he, 'Kippur.'

'By George, I mean to say by Arthur, I mean to say by Henry Campbell-Bannerman, I mean to say by Henry Asquith, later Earl of Oxford, God rest his great soul, excuse me, Sir, I feel deeply about these things – after all something has to be sacred, doesn't it, Chief? – you're a Hades of a one (if I do not commit some solecism by confusing the Greek conception of the after-life with that of the Jews, these latter being currently on the conference agenda). What you mean is, we did should ought to have a story, kind of exclusive in its human-interest way, about Yom Kippur?'

'It was', replied Lord Northcliffe, who was already contemplating the purchase of *The Times*, 'the thought which had flitted through what I always call my mind.'

'Great, Chief!' assented the acting editor and temporary bootblack.

Missing the comma, the scheduled Lord, still way back in the first decade after the bend of the century had been successfully rounded, took such violent exception that he was on the verge of sending for the future Lord Rothermere, who was still thinking about *Tit-bits*. 'Why you-all call me – me big sitting democrat, interest people at heart – "great Chief"? Bad medicine. Opposition are going to call it feudal.'

'I had', said the man, with a sinking heart, 'a comma in there. May I explain?'

'Never explain, never apologize!' replied the controversial figure, putting the phrase squarely on the journalistic map.

After that, things moved along at a very fair clip, it being realized by the English that a boy who could not face the papers was unlikely to be able to face the facts. Incidentally, it should be mentioned here that research has clarified what Wilhelm II, Kaiser, and a German if ever there was one (the fellow was, after all, like so many others, a grandson of Queen Victoria), meant when, in his notorious attack on what he impudently referred to as *Englische Propaganda Luegen und Nordcliffsche Atrocitaets Erfindungen im bald-kommenden Weltkrieg* (his high-flown term for the little bulletins of the English Information Service of World War I), he spoke of the 'Contemptible Little Army'.

Fusiliers bristled at the rumour that the term applied to them. Two Divisions of the incomparable French

Army (later under Foch, pronounced fossch) but at that time under Joffre, threatened a sympathetic mutiny, regardless of the imminent menace of the Boche (pronounced at the time bossch). 'Huns' and 'international solidarity of the working class in face of the on-rush of imperialist war' were also terms currently on the lips of the soldiery everywhere, a situation of which Lenin was not slow to take advantage.

Not a moment too soon, though several years too late, ex-Kaiser Bill issued from Doorn his famous statement. 'Bloody iron,' he cried ('between ourselves', remarked the interpreter, His Late All-Highest Majesty never fully "dug" Bismarck'), 'I was talking about the journalistic army. Take that big organ, *The Times*. It does but express the views of a limited, and, in my estimation, doomed section of the 'Top' class which can scarcely hope to survive the world conflagration that seems to be on. In any case, I withdrew the phrase unreservedly.'

'Oh, hang the Kaiser!' was Northcliffe's very natural reaction to that, and at Versailles, Lloyd George – still smarting under Wilson's suggestion that he did not know where Przemysl was – took up the cry. The influence of the press had not been in vain.

Yet once again, the press was in a dilemma. Used, as it was, to roughing it, the constant drip-drip of the quandary, the monotonous diet of haughty censoriousness, money, vulgar disbelief and money, could wear out the strongest nerves. If a paper failed to make money it was accused of being at the best an effete survival of an earlier age, failing now to meet the demands of a new, eager generation caring little for Aristotle and less for Milton's *Areopagitica*; and at the worst an out-of-touch mess.

If it made, on the other hand, money – and, in fairness to future men like the future Lord Beaverbrook, it must be said that accusations of poverty, garret-living, lack of wherewithal, 'Where's the brass?' and irresponsible indifference to the profitability of a given enterprise were unfounded – people said that it was making money. And that, they said, was not what the press was supposed to be for. On the contrary, it was supposed to be something between the prophet Elijah and that cousin of Mr Gladstone who was so disinterested and selfless that he refused to judge a beauty competition at Brighton on the ground that it might somehow gain him publicity and thus 'improper' influence.

And if it was not one of these things it was another. Either the man was a press Baron, evil *per se*, or he was under the influence, evil *per se*, of the advertisers. If there were a lot of advertisers, they were running the paper in their own interests, getting (it was reported to the 1926 Commission of Enquiry) advertisements for spavined motor-cycles inserted in places where they would subtly influence students of form for the Gold Cup. Or there were less and less advertisers, in which case what confidence could the public have in the acumen of a man who on the one hand claimed to know the right course to adopt as regards housing, the Caribbean, and the bad situation seen to be developing in Hongkong, and on the other seemed to have lost the confidence of the man at Shell who had the final say-so about the advertising budget?

Small wonder that English newspaper owners – they were termed at this time 'Barons' to frighten the unsophisticated – became moody and irritable. The first Baron Beaverbrook toyed with the idea of putting a bit of a jerk into the Empire. The first Baron Rothermere toyed with the idea of putting some jerk on to the throne of Hungary – the office boy was the fellow he had in mind, and plans were drawn showing the exact position of Hungary on the map of Europe. They even found Przemysl, living under another name.

The first Baron Southwood, whom some of his fellow Barons at first erroneously supposed to be a bit of a jerk because, while they were straining themselves to plot, with champagne and experts, in Rome, Cairo and Montreal, he would never go further than a small club-orange in the Palm Court at Bournemouth, thus stealing an unfair advantage, took one look at the situation and went back, as many an honest Englishman has, to Caxton.

He reasoned thus: 'Caxton had a printing press. So have I, or at least Odham's Ltd has. Caxton was not doing so well as he could have wished. Nor, between you, me and the gatepost, are Odhams. Caxton said "What's the stuff people are really going for? The Bible isn't it, you chaps?" I said, "What's the thing people are really going for? Bit of progress, Labour etc. etc., isn't it, you chaps?" Caxton said, "So let's print

Caxton's Bible." Mind you there were people there who had no bold imaginative spirit. And as for the pay-off value of a bit of moral leadership, they were – what was the word the man used? You've got it in one – they were purblind. They said, purblindly, that there was a whole lot of stuff in the Bible that would scare off the advertisers. David and Uriah, they shouted, and criticisms of that carping character. "Call this a Family Bible," they said, "I've got a press and I'm going to keep it pressing. With a gift-scheme if necessary." And I said "I've got a press, and I'm going to keep it turning'. "

The results were the *Daily Herald*, the *Tatler & Bystander*, the *People*, *Debrett's*, *Illustrated* – and others, too numerous for individual mention, but all excellent.

The loud, clear voice of Labour, pointing England's way forward without fear or favour, while still recognizing that in this country Rome is not built in a day and, unlike a certain type of continental doctrinaire, we do not let go of one dividend until we have latched on to another, was heard in the land.

The early and erstwhile pioneers of Free Speech, after brief and successful consultation as to what you do when you wish to indicate that turning in your grave is the opposite of what you are doing, and that you are, on the contrary, absolutely delighted with the way everything is moving onwards and upwards like Milton envisaged it, sent a message of congratulation and encouragement.

'I take this', Mr Ernest Bevin is reported to have said on receiving it, 'as a message of congratulation and encouragement.'

'Looks like it to me,' said Arthur ('Lido') Lansbury.

On the motion of the Secretary it was agreed to strike from the record the name of Daniel Defoe, on the ground that he was a natural-born crypto-this or crypto-that, Left, Right or Centre, unlikely to redound to the credit of the Party and susceptible of alienating the upper, middle or working classes according to the taste prevailing at the moment. The moving little tribute from the glorious past was then accepted with unanimity.

But, as the poet has said, 'English history saith an ending to all good things must be', and just as it looked as though Progress had got used to her new surroundings and was even prepared to spell out a few simple words like 'rent-decontrol-stabilisation-personnel', the tabliod press – headed by the *Daily Mirror* with a *posse* of shareholders the more sinister in that they were masked – broke in at the rear of the establishment and, while one said, 'If nobody moves, nobody's going to get hurt, much,' removed a portion of the year's takings.

'Is nothing sacred?' asked a man at Transport House.

And thus the English press, with its long tradition, started what was confidently hoped, as the Chairman of the Board said at the inaugural dinner, would be another long tradition.

Asked to sum up his impressions of the situation, its significance and probable ultimate outcome, Lord Attlee is alleged to have said (not, it goes without saying, for the record) that it was 'all very interesting'.

A GOOD TIME HAD

CONCLUDING, as is customary at some point, this survey of our very full and varied national history, much of it grown on our own home farm, one can hardly improve upon the dictum of Pringle, probably the greatest of English historians, when asked to evaluate the course of events. 'It might', he pronounced, 'have been a bloody sight worse.'

(We are not, of course, referring to Sir John Pringle who, though in 1752 he married the daughter of Dr William Oliver of Bath, known to his intimates as 'Bath' Oliver, in jocular allusion to a large, thinnish biscuit of unusual design and flavour, was not an historian at all but a doctor who devoted much of his time to examining how horribly diseased people in the Army were, and why. Nor should either of these Pringles be confused with the notorious P 'pander' Pringle, so-called by his intimates in jocular allusion to his profession.)

Even the third Marquess of Salisbury, though he had once ventured to describe English policy as one of 'bounce and baseness' is believed secretly to have agreed with Pringle's considered estimate. (The

Marquess was, of course, a sceptic, of whom it has been said that it is doubtful whether he knew even how to spell 'democracy', let alone do it.)

It goes without saying that there have been those who, from time to time, saw room for improvement. They tended, however, to be discredited by association in the public mind with Karl Marx who was not only German, and mistaken on a number of points, but did not scruple to publish an attack, in odious taste, upon Mr Levy, at that time proprietor of the *Daily Telegraph*. Since later *critiques* of Marxism were not at his disposal, Mr Levy had no effective means of defending himself, a circumstance which rendered the attack all the more petty and, as Gladstone said at the time, 'somehow un-English'.

Although, when viewed from the standpoint of what the late Maynard Keynes described as 'those sad-faced men who look as though they had done badly out of the wars', English history may seem to have been going on for a long time, there is still probably a good deal to come. In any case, it is a mistake to make arbitrary divisions between what may be termed 'vintage' history and the newer models. The expression 'Twentieth century' is in itself an arbitrary division. Those who state vaguely that it all started with the Education Acts of the 1870's, are, the late Lord Balbour was wont to insist, 'talking loosely'.

'I abhor loose talk above all things,' commented the late Lord Baldwin. The ensuing dialogue then ensued:

Lord B: 'Don't we all?'

Lord B: 'Don't we all what?'

Lord B: 'What you said.'

Lord B: 'Have it your own way, bearing in mind that the country's resources are not limitless.'

(It was this carelessly phrased *caveat* which gained Lord B a reputation for defeatism and undemocratic thinking, with the result that before he was very much older people were saying exactly the same thing about him that they had said about Lord Salisbury.)

And the fact remains that Moody and Sankey, the American evangelists, did not set foot in England until the spring of 1875, the Railway Jubilee at Darlington opened no earlier than September of the same year, and it was *not until the middle of the year following* that an unprecedented drought and heat-wave brought ruin to fruit-farmers in many parts of the country.

In other words, anyone under the impression that any one thing caused anything is not seeing history 'in the round'. He is probably not even facing it squarely, and might well incur the censure of a former Archbishop of York who, in a phase parts of which are unfortunately unprintable, remarked that 'a lot of these . . . s strike me as being round the . . . bend'.

The Government of the day agreed with him, and his views did much to lay the foundations of what later came to be known as the Concert of Europe, Benelux, Nato, Shape, Snafu and the public opinion of enlightened people.

By hindsight it is, of course, possible to see that the real turning point was probably Lord Rosebery, sometimes called 'Nature's Welfare State'. This is in reference to the fact that by marrying a Rothschild, being Prime Minister and winning the Derby, he demonstrated that it was possible to improve one's financial status and run the Empire without neglecting the study of form. It was a thought which sustained many an Englishman in many a dark hour. It showed that there was still room at the top. It is, however, doubtful whether he actually said that he would rather win the Derby than be Prime Minister, or merely pretended to have said it, as being a suitably English phrase which people could easily remember and quote whenever Prime Ministers or the Derby were mentioned. He may, however, have said that he would rather win the 2.30 at Alexandra Park than be Minister of Works.

Saying things has always been a characteristic habit of the more important sort of English statesmen. Cromwell, as we have seen, did it repeatedly. The late Lord Haldane said 'Germany is my spiritual home', thus thoughtlessly wrecking his career when the first world war broke out. The late Lord Baldwin said 'the bomber will always get through' but resigned soon afterwards. The practice, however, remains popular, though, in these modern days, confined chiefly to Airports, going and coming.

Professor Manx, of Zürich, to whose kindness and unflagging industry I am indebted for a number of criticisms of this study, though in the event none of them has proved of any value, has suggested that to some readers the survey may appear to begin or end a little too soon or a little too late. 'How silly can you get?' was the comment of Professor Sodor of the Sarbonne on being shown this egregious communication from the sage of Zürich. (With his unflagging industry and kindness Professor Sodor undertook to read the book in manuscript and make such suggestions and corrections as might be necessary. Mis-statements, omissions of vital facts, contradictions, feeble construction, poor organization of material, slipshod writing, woolly thinking and errors of judgment and taste are, therefore, his responsibility.)

It is not merely hard to see what Manx meant, but even what he thought he meant. Sodor was like that, too.

In any case it may be remarked that to conclude a survey of English history with, for example, the death of Edward the Confessor – important though it may have seemed at the time – would have involved the omission of much that is of interest to overseas visitors. On the other hand, to continue it, as some have suggested, to, for example, the moment of the vital London conference of 1960 (itself the natural sequel to the events of 1959) would make tedious reading for those who have already formed a pretty comprehensive view of what is going to happen next, yet could scarcely hope to engage the attention of others who, in the words of the late Humbert Wolfe, prefer to 'greet the unseen with a sneer'.

'Ever think much about posterity?' the late Edward VII is reported to have asked the late Lord Balfour in the course of one of what the latter was wont to describe as 'those bull sessions' at Homburg.

'Can't say I have,' replied Lord B, absent-mindedly watching the graceful movements of a famous Edwardian beauty who at this moment entered the famed Casino where Russian Grand Dukes vied with Austrian Archdukes in dancing on, as was then the popular pastime, the edge of a volcano.

'Sire!' said the King sharply.

'Eh?' ejaculated the bemused statesman.

'Say "Sire" when you speak to me' snapped the monarch. 'Just because I – We, to put it bluntly – know how to unbend, there's no call for you to take liberties.'

In an effort to divert the course of a conversation which had become dangerous, Lord Balfour remarked chattily that he had that very morning been re-reading Mill on Liberty and considered it 'fearful tosh'.

Mollified, his royal master passed the remark that

'the trouble with posterity is you never know whether it's going to be worth our having done anything for it or not'.

'Might turn out a scruffy lot, you mean? Sire.'

'Or not, of course. Mustn't jump to conclusions.'

'Just speculating,' replied the other, 'I have a speculative second nature. Second nature to me to speculate.'

'If you don't speculate, you can't accumulate,' laughed the 'peace-maker', and suiting the action to the word, strove to lead his companion of the week towards the baccarat rooms, where a second cousin of the Tzar who had never heard of Kerensky, not to mention Lenin, Stalin, Malenkov, that man just behind Bulganin in the *Time* picture, or Kruschev, was staking – recklessly, as some men even at that date did not hesitate to hint – the whole Black Sea Fleet on the turn of a card. Stanley Baldwin, who later became an Earl because of the way things went, was present as a comparatively young man, and pronounced the action 'reckless'.

'That Grand Duke', observed Lord Balfour, 'is fiddling at baccarat while Rome burns.'

The King, glancing at him 'suspiciously' (if we are to accept Prince Bismarck's account of the incident) said 'We do not care for talk of fiddling at baccarat.'

'No indeed, Sire,' acknowledged the Scottish scion, who was practising for later triumphs in America. 'Mind, by the way, the volcano.'

'What volcano, you fuddy-duddy old alarmist you?' queried Edward, the shape of whose trousers – creased sideways instead of fore-and-aft – was alone enough to earn him the respectful glances of the cosmopolitan crowd in which jostling had been carried to new heights of refinement. A well known Parisian cocotte was actually seen jostling the shade of Turgeniev who was hurrying to avoid lending yet another thousand rubles to the shade of Dostoyevsky, the hectic pallor on whose cheeks indicated only too clearly his fever of uncertainty as to whether he was going to be scheduled as the greatest man since Pushkin, the kiss of death, or rehabilitated in a nation-wide illustrated edition.

At this point a comparatively young man, possibly either the future Lord Baldwin, the future Lord Attlee, or somebody entirely different who, if he ever had a role to play, must have left it in the cab – it all depends upon the date of this incident, and whether it took place in Homburg or Aix-en-Provence, a point which only painstaking research could establish, which makes it scarcely worth while – stumbled up and asked the grandfather of him who, at no distant date, was to become Edward VIII, for his autograph 'in the interests of posterity'.

'Generations yet unborn, sort of thing, what?' smiled the ever-gracious ruler of what Lord Balfour had once dubbed 'the biggest thing since Rome'. (And it must be noted that, when Lord Balfour dubbed, he dubbed with a will.)

'Well, as for me,' moodily admitted the youngster, 'I'm a pessimist.'

'Nonsense!' cried Lord Balfour, in a rare access of irritation. 'These are halcyon days. Carefree. Not a cloud, apparently, that is to say, on the international horizon. England at the height of her power – and that goes for you too, you whiskered horror,' he remarked *sotto voce* to the comparatively youthful Admiral von Tirpitz who had seated himself at a nearby table where he was boisterously entertaining a gay crowd of posterity including Admiral Canaris, General Guderian, and the ever-popular banker-to-be Hjalmar Schacht, who, amid laughing acclaim, had declared himself ready to 'foot the bill' in the interests of western civilization.

'Talk about *parvenus*,' a backward-looking Englishman remarked to a backward-looking Frenchman. 'And who, may I ask,' he added, 'on earth are those two fellows?'

'Think I've got eyes in the back of my head?' enquired the Frenchman – a man named Esterhazy who had come to the place for health reasons – testily. However, through these luminous though retroactive orbs he was able to note the shade of Napoleon Bonaparte in eager argument with the spectre of Adolf Hitler.

'One of them's that fellow Rosebery knows of,' said Lord Balfour. 'Can't place the other chap at all. Both look like a couple of corporals to me'.

'We get them here going and coming,' ventured the *doyen* of European *hôteliers* who had been surveying the animated scene, 'one going, one coming'.

With his never-failing tact and prescience, Edward (or 'Teddy' as he was affectionately known to millions of his subjects) interrupted to greet on his arrival at the place, and to pay a well-judged meed of homage to Theodore (or 'Teddy' as he was affectionately known to millions of his fellow-countrymen, Republicans and Democrats alike, who saw in him a symbol of national unity and progress at a time when the old party machines were failing to satisfy the aspirations of a people in whose character a rugged dollar-awareness is blended with a rare degree of idealism and mother-love) Roosevelt, who had just bust a Trust.

After some well-judged comments on the American statesman's physical and mental vigour and abounding vitality, Lord Balfour, at a nudge from the King, saw his opportunity to pave the way for posterity by enquiring of his Yankee *vis-à-vis*, 'I say, old sport, got any money on you? We're skint, as they say in dear ould Oireland whence so many of your urban voters derive?'

Anglo-American relations had taken a step forward.

'That's surely not *the* Roosevelt?' questioned a future Chancellor of the Exchequer, not without a certain apprehension.

'No, no, the other one.'

'Oh goody!'

'Wait for it, buddy,' warned his kindly mentor, 'F.D.R. isn't going to be the end of the line, not by a long chalk'.

A Russian, who was talking to another Russian about Trotsky in general, now said to that other: 'By the way, in particular, how's Bronstein?'

'Playing chess,' said the other, 'so far as I understand, in the Bronx, waiting for the moment when, after a dash home and get-together with Vladimir Ulyanov, known to you as Lenin, he may well take over the Government of our great country.'

'Baccarat here, chess there,' vouchsafed the other philosophically. 'Way the world goes sort of business. And by the way, isn't that Djugaschveli over there – chap with the big moustache and, as I live and breathe, his suit all awry from the way the pistols drag it down? It is, it is he. Hi-ya, Djugaschveli, how's it go?'

The character so addressed emitted a slow snarl. 'Listen,' snarled he, 'a bit less of this Djuga stuff. I'm a man from Georgia, of limited horizons. I'm not supposed ever to have been outside Russia except when I went, that one time, to London with that fellow Lenin who, I don't mind telling you, if you care to hear the story, doesn't want me to be his successor. The things he says about me – calls me Stalin, and then laughs in that not-so-funny way he has – you'd hardly credit. You let on I'm over here at the tables, they'll all have a red fit. I keep telling you, I'm a strictly Georgian hermit – don't understand the first thing about Abroad.'

'Mum's the word,' loyally replied the friend of Bronstein. 'May I call you Joe?'

'No law against it – yet' replied the Georgian.

'Good-oh,' cried the other, 'and what a sunset.' Moved by the beauty of nature he sprang towards King Edward VII and, in an access of general goodwill, cried: 'Comrade, may I call you comrade?'

'It looks to me' observed Lord Balfour, to the bearded figure beside him, 'Sire, a little as though modern history, as we are wont to term it for lack of a more specific classification, were about to begin.'